# Dyslexia

RESOURCE MATERIALS FOR TEACHERS

# Dyslexia

## A Practical Guide for Teachers and Parents

**Barbara Riddick, Judith Wolfe
and David Lumsdon**

**David Fulton Publishers**
London

David Fulton Publishers Ltd
The Chiswick Centre, 414 Chiswick High Road, London W4 5TF

www.fultonpublishers.co.uk

First published in Great Britain in 2002 by David Fulton Publishers

Reprinted 2003
10 9 8 7 6 5 4 3 2

*British Library Cataloguing in Publication Data*
A catalogue record for this book is available from the British Library.

ISBN 1–85346–780–4

Typeset by Mark Heslington, Scarborough, North Yorkshire
Printed and bound in Great Britain by Ashford Colour Press Limited, Gosport, Hants

# Contents

# Acknowledgements

We would like to thank Elizabeth Henderson, head of Oldfield Primary and Infant School, for her valuable contribution.

We would also like to thank all the children, parents and teachers who gave us their views.

We would also like to acknowledge the contribution to this book and to the success of pupils made by all the staff of Saint Wilfrid's RC Comprehensive School.

# Chapter 1

# Defining and Identifying Dyslexia

*Dyslexia* comes from the Greek

$$Dys \; = \; impaired$$
$$+$$
$$Lexia \; = \; word$$

Recent definitions of dyslexia such as the one produced by a working party of the British Psychological Society (1999) endorse the original meaning of the word dyslexia by emphasising the difficulties with individual words.

> *Dyslexia is evident when accurate and fluent word reading and/or spelling develops very incompletely or with great difficulty. This focuses on literacy learning at the 'word level' and implies the problem is severe and persistent despite appropriate learning opportunities.*

Berninger (2001) underlines the point that in dyslexia there is a discrepancy between impaired individual word skills and adequate or good higher level skills such as verbal reasoning and text comprehension. For this reason many schools and psychologists now look at the relationship between reading comprehension and reading rate and accuracy or at the relationship between listening and reading comprehension. Dyslexic children invariably score better on reading comprehension than on reading rate and accuracy and better on listening comprehension as opposed to reading comprehension.

Critics have noted that this is a rather limited definition which does not specify the range of literacy and other difficulties encountered or the underlying processing impairments which lead to these difficulties or differences.

Understanding the basis of definitions of dyslexia is

important because it will give teachers insight into children that they have found puzzling and unusual in their uneven range of talents and difficulties.

Everyone has a cognitive profile – a range of thinking, perceptual and memory processing skills which are unique to them. We all have relative strengths and weaknesses in our cognitive profiles but overall most of our skills will fall in the normal range. Where somebody has difficulty with the majority of these processing skills as manifested by very restricted learning and day-to-day living skills they are deemed in Britain to have a severe learning disability. When an individual has difficulties or impairments in just one or two areas in contrast to average or good skills especially in abstract reasoning, judgement, problem solving, etc. this is deemed a specific learning difficulty.

## *Specific learning difficulty*

Specific learning difficulty or SpLD is a generic term as there are a range of different types of SpLDs. A child may have coordination problems and be identified as dyspraxic, or have specific difficulties with numbers but not literacy, in which case they may be termed dyscalculic.

**Dyslexia** is the most common type of SpLD identified at present, and a proportion of educationalists and policy makers use the term SpLD instead of dyslexia. Some educationalists argue that a number of children have difficulties which overlap more than one category of specific learning difficulty or have specific learning difficulties that do not seem to fit any of the familiar categories. Partly for these reasons they prefer to use the term specific learning difficulty.

Despite some reservations about the term dyslexia in educational circles it is gaining ground and is now recognised in government and professional publications (e.g. DfEE 1997, British Psychological Society 1999, DfES 2001). Research with dyslexic children and their parents shows that they clearly prefer the term dyslexia. From a social or environmental perspective this is understandable. The term dyslexia allows them to access or identify with support organisations, specialist literature, role models, specialist programmes or IT and others with similar difficulties.

Miles and Miles (1999) have pointed out the difficulty in trying to formulate a definition of what is a complex syndrome which varies from person to person with not all indicators present in all individuals with dyslexia. They also note that different definitions of dyslexia are constructed by varying social groups for different purposes and we would add also for different historical circumstances.

One of the oldest and in its time most influential definitions of dyslexia was provided by the World Federation of Neurology in 1968.

> *Dyslexia is a disorder manifested in difficulty learning to read despite conventional instruction, adequate intelligence and socio-cultural opportunity. It is dependent on fundamental cognitive disabilities which are frequently constitutional in origin.*

This definition was of its time in countering the widely held assumptions that children who didn't learn to read were either poorly educated or failed to learn to read because of lack of intelligence. It stressed the constitutional nature of dyslexia and paved the way for a considerable explosion of research on the cognitive difficulties underlying dyslexia.

The definition also emphasised the reading difficulty aspect of dyslexia, probably because this was often the first noticeable difficulty to arise for a child. More recent definitions emphasise that dyslexia affects many aspects of literacy including spelling and writing and also other skills such as numeracy and sometimes motor coordination. The following definition by the British Dyslexia Association (in Peer 1994) lists a range of difficulties:

> *A combination of abilities and difficulties which affect the learning process in one or more of reading, spelling and writing. Accompanying weaknesses may be identified in areas of speed of processing, short term memory, sequencing, auditory and/or visual perception, spoken language and motor skills. It is particularly related to mastering written language, which may include alphabetic, numeric and musical notation. (p. 68)*

Definitions of this sort specify to a greater or lesser extent the underlying processing difficulties which lead to problems with skills such as reading, writing and spelling.

Because dyslexia can affect a wide range of seemingly disparate tasks such as copying from the board, tying up shoelaces and remembering multiplication tables, as well as the more obvious literacy tasks, it is important to understand a little about the underlying cognitive or processing difficulties. The advantage of this is that teachers can then work out or anticipate what kind of tasks may challenge some of the dyslexic children they encounter. It also enables them to think out ways of circumventing the difficulty or helping the child to cope with it. On a more positive note it also helps the teacher to identify what activities or parts of activities the child might be good at.

## Short-term or working memory

Inefficient *short-term* or *working memory* has long been implicated as one of the underlying factors in dyslexia (McLoughlin *et al.* 1994, Beech 1997, Singleton 1999). Many dyslexic children perform less well on digit span tasks than non-dyslexic children. These involve asking a child to repeat a series of numbers either forwards or backwards:

Please say after me 5 8 3 7 5 2

Short-term or working memory is used to hold new information briefly in mind, such as telephone numbers or the name of someone we have just been introduced to. It is not hard to imagine a whole range of difficulties that may possibly emerge for the child in the classroom:

*Remembering*
- numbers while doing mental arithmetic;
- new subject words;
- verbal instructions;
- words on board to copy down (child has to look up far more frequently than other children).

Each child is different and children can develop coping strategies so it is important to observe how this affects individual children.

## Automaticity

As well as short-term memory difficulties dyslexic children also have difficulty in transferring some types of information from their short-term to long-term memory. They seem to need many more exposures on average before they can remember for example someone's name or how a certain word is spelt. This particularly affects rote learning of sequences of words or numbers, such as:

- days of the week;
- months of the year;
- the alphabet;
- multiplication tables;
- counting to ten.

*A 5-year-old dyslexic boy was asked what 3 plus 4 made. He replied what's that number after 6 called? His mother confirmed that he still had difficulty counting to 10 but seemed to understand how numbers worked.*

This underlines the point that a child can have good conceptual ability, they can solve the problem or task as long as their particular input or output difficulties are circumvented.

Fawcett and Nicolson (1992) demonstrated that dyslexic

children could count backwards as well as other children and walk along a balance beam as well as other children, but when they were asked to count backwards while walking along a balance beam, their balancing performance deteriorated significantly compared to other children. They suggest this indicates that counting backwards and balancing are both less 'automatic' for dyslexic children and that these take more of their concentration and attention than for non-dyslexic children. The advantage of being able to do some tasks automatically is that it leaves more of a child's processing abilities free to concentrate on new or higher order tasks. Thus lack of automaticity, particularly in literacy and numeracy skills, means that dyslexic children are more likely to encounter processing overload when asked to carry out new or complex tasks in the classroom. Automaticity can affect a wide range of skills, including various motor skills such as:

- tying up shoelaces;
- catching a ball;
- skipping;
- handwriting;
- swimming.

Some leading dyslexia researchers like Snowling (1995) and Lundberg and Hoien (2001) have proposed that phonological processing difficulties are fundamental to dyslexia and are found to a greater or lesser degree in all individuals with dyslexia. Phonemes are the smallest detectable sound elements that words can be divided up into. Some children have greater difficulty in detecting these phonemes and particular difficulty in linking phonemes to graphemes (written sound representations). The following are all indicators of phonological difficulties:

*Phonological processing difficulties*

- problems in segmenting words into phonemes;
- problems keeping strings of sounds or letters in short-term memory;
- problems repeating back long non-words;
- problems in reading or writing non-words;
- slow naming of colours, numbers, letters and objects in pictures;
- a slower rate of speech, sometimes with indistinct pronunciation;
- problems in playing word games where the idea is to manipulate phonemes.

(from Lundberg and Hoien 2001: 109)

Non-words are words that do not currently exist in the English language but could plausibly do so, e.g. *wub, grimskit*.

Researchers have found them a useful way of investigating children's phonological skills because children cannot use visual cues or familiarity with the word to help them decide how to read or spell it. Dyslexic children often use their stronger semantic skills to help them decode words in written text. Tests of non-word reading and spelling are now widely used in assessing for dyslexia (Snowling *et al.* 1996).

A number of studies have found that children who have delayed or weak phonological processing skills are more likely to encounter difficulties in learning to read and spell. Because of the weight of evidence on the importance of children developing good early phonological skills this has become a central part of the National Literacy Strategy and the Literacy Hour. Phonological awareness is now taught to all children during their first years of schooling.

## *Visual difficulties and the magnocellular system*

### Visual perceptual difficulties

These are difficulties in how visual information, particularly of a written nature, is initially perceived. A small percentage of dyslexic children report that words on the printed page can appear fuzzy or blurred or jump around even though they seem to have normal vision. Garzia (1993), in a review of the literature, concluded that in a minority of children optical difficulties did seem to play a part in their delayed reading. These difficulties were related to a wide range of less obvious visual factors such as poor binocular vision or poor eye movement control. It is suggested that especially where a child reports discomfort or odd visual experiences while reading, they should be given a comprehensive visual assessment.

### Visual processing difficulties

There has been considerable debate as to whether visual difficulties such as unstable binocular vision are indicative of difficulties in the visual magnocellular system or pathway of dyslexics. There are two pathways by which information is passed from the eyes to the brain:

1. Magnocellular pathway–transient channel enabling flicker or rapid change detection.
2. Parvocellular pathway–sustained channel enabling detection of stationary detailed patterns.

Researchers have found that dyslexic children compared to non-dyslexic children do worse at tasks like flicker detection that test the efficiency of their transient channel but equally as well on tasks that test their sustained channel.

Stein and Walsh (1997) have suggested that rather than seeing visual or phonological or motor difficulties as alternative or opposing explanations for dyslexia they may all be indicative of an underlying temporal or timing difficulty: 'Rather temporal processing in all three systems seems to be impaired. Dyslexics may be unable to process fast incoming sensory information adequately in any domain' (Stein and Walsh 1997: 147).

## *Temporal or timing difficulties*

Frith and Frith (1996) pointed out that in order to distinguish between phonemes (speech sounds) in ongoing speech, individuals have to be able to detect rapid changes in auditory frequencies. They also endorse the idea that fundamental difficulties in timing may underlie dyslexia. Fawcett and Nicolson (2001) have proposed that deficits in the cerebellum may account for the automatisation difficulties that dyslexic children display in many different areas of skill. They speculate that different sub-types within dyslexia may have different underlying deficits or differences in brain function.

This is still an active area of research and debate but a clearer understanding of why dyslexia seems to affect such a pervasive range of activities is beginning to emerge. This is of relevance to practitioners in alerting them to the wide range of subtle and not so subtle ways in which dyslexic children may have difficulties. It underlines the importance of not viewing dyslexia simply as a literacy difficulty but appreciating that some aspects of motor and organisational skills as well as numeracy may be affected. It also emphasises that processing speed is often a critical issue for individuals with dyslexia. On a range of cognitive tasks they take longer than non-dyslexics. This difference is often measured in milliseconds for individual responses but the cumulative effect is that they need more time to learn or process information or output their response. On a number of tasks dyslexics can perform as well as non-dyslexics if given sufficient time. At the same time it has to be emphasised that it is only transient processing that is affected and that dyslexics have good sustained processing systems which allow them to perform many cognitive tasks as proficiently as non-dyslexics. The reason for reading being particularly affected is that it requires highly efficient and accurate processing at extremely high speed (Wolf and O'Brien 2001).

### The strengths of dyslexia

Singleton (1999) says that we should be wary about automatically assuming that cognitive differences are inevitably deficits. Some of the cognitive differences that dyslexic children display may actually confer advantages for some kinds of thinking or encourage them to find alternative routes to learning: 'The deficit model of dyslexia is now steadily giving way to one in which dyslexia is increasingly recognised as a difference in cognition and learning' (Singleton 1999: 27).

The following are some of the strengths that individuals with dyslexia may display:

- inquiring mind;
- problem solving;
- comprehending new ideas;
- generating ideas;
- analytic thinking;
- creative thinking;
- 3-D constructions;
- finding different strategies;
- seeing the 'big picture';
- insightful thinking.

The important point is that strategies are devised which allow these good conceptual and creative higher order thinking skills to be expressed and appreciated in the classroom.

*Ben is 17 years of age and is taking science A levels including maths and further maths. He is severely dyslexic but has had individual support since the age of 8 years. At primary school dyslexia in general was not recognised and the one-to-one specialist support he received was out of school time. His severe literacy difficulties led to him being very anxious and demoralised. His secondary school provided good out-of-class and within-class support with the majority of subject teachers having a sympathetic attitude. As a consequence his self-esteem and confidence improved considerably. Teachers across all areas of the curriculum commented on his quick grasp of new ideas and undoubted conceptual ability. Whereas support in the early years had focused on systematic phonological teaching and literacy skills, support during the GCSE years focused on study skills and organisation. He attended an evening class in order to improve his keyboard skills. In written areas of the curriculum he was allowed to word process homework and later on, GCSE course work. He was given help with note taking and the organisation and presentation of his work. His English teacher was particularly supportive and praised the originality of his writing, which in turn improved his motivation and led to him achieving A\*s in both GCSE English language and literature. He was allowed extra time in his GCSEs and a word processor where appropriate. He gained excellent GCSE and AS level grades and has been offered places at several leading universities to study science. His A level teachers consider him to have an original and outstanding scientific mind and a flair for mathematics although he still cannot recite his multiplication tables. Although reading is still slow and effortful he reads for pleasure and enjoys creative writing.*

Figure 1.1 shows an example of Ben's writing at 7 years of age before he received any specialist teaching. In Figure 1.2 is an example of Ben's writing at 10 years of age after four years of specialist teaching. He had been taught cursive handwriting but found it impossible to cope with so had to revert to printing.

## Incidence of dyslexia

Both Miles and Miles (1999) and the British Dyslexia Association (in Peer 1994) claim that:

- up to 4 per cent of children have severe dyslexia;
- up to 10 per cent of children have milder dyslexia-type difficulties.

On average a teacher might expect to have one severely dyslexic child in their class although in reality this fluctuates considerably. There is no link between either dyslexia and social class or dyslexia and ability, as children from across the social class range and the ability range are equally likely to have dyslexia. Until recently it was claimed that boys were four to five times more likely to have dyslexia than girls. Recent research has queried whether girls are under-identified because they are less likely to draw attention to themselves by acting out their frustrations and anxieties and perhaps because adults have lower expectations of encountering dyslexic girls. This is still an unresolved issue but does suggest that practitioners should be on the lookout for dyslexic girls.

*Dyslexia and bilingualism*

Another area of concern had been the under-identification of dyslexia in children from multilingual and bilingual backgrounds (Deponio *et al.* 2000). Until recently it was often assumed that if such children were not making progress in reading and writing English then this could be attributed to English being their second language. Deponio *et al.* (2000) made two key recommendations:

- children should be assessed in their first language;
- first language assessment should be supplemented by classroom observations of non-literacy-based tasks such as motor skills, organisational skills and thinking skills.

Kelly (2002) of Park Dean School in Oldham stresses the importance of talking to the parents of bilingual children and finding out how they use language at home.

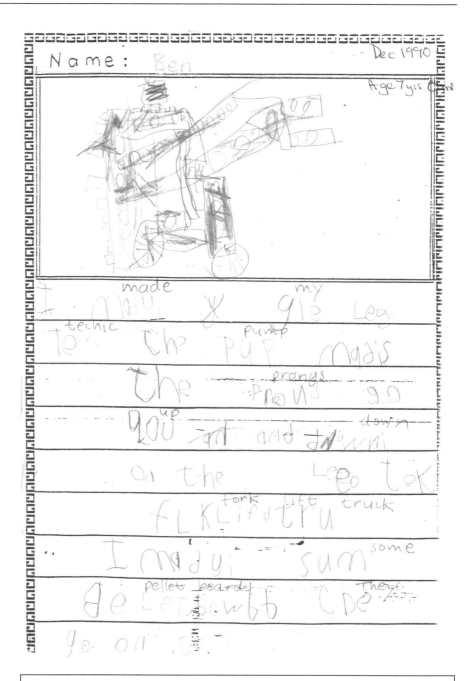

I made my lego technic.
The pump makes the prongs
go up and down on the lego
technic forklift truck.
I made some pellet boards
they go on it.

**Figure 1.1** Ben aged 7 years – unaided writing in class

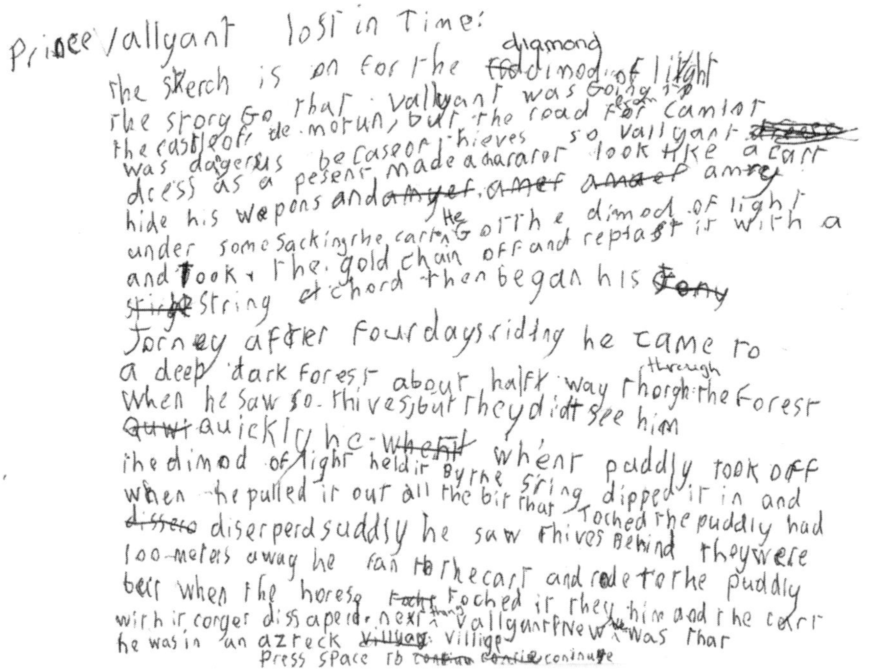

Prince Vallyant lost in Time:
the skerch is on for the diamond of light
the story go that Vallyant was going to
the castle of de Montun, but the road for Camlot
was dagerus becase of thieves so Vallyant
dcess as a pesent made a chararer look like a cart
hide his wepons and armer under some sacking the cart
He or the dimod of light
and took + the gold chain off and replast it with a
string et chord then began his
jorney after four days ridtng he came to
a deep dark forest about half way thorgh the Forest
When he saw so thives but they didt see him
quickly he went
the dimod of light heidit by the sring and dipped it in and
when he pulled it out all the bit that toched the puddiy had
diserperd suddiy he saw thives behind they were
100 meters away he ran to the cart and rode to the puddiy
becs when the horese toched it they him and the cart
with it corger dissaperd next Vallyant New was that
he was in an azteck Villige
Press space to coninue

---

## Prince Valiant lost in Time

The search is on for the diamond of light. The story goes that Valiant was going to the Castle of de Montford, but the road from Camelot to the castle was dangerous because of thieves. So Valiant dressed as a peasant and made a chariot look like a cart. He hid his weapons and armour under some sacking in the cart. He got the diamond of light and took the gold chain off and replaced it with strong cord. Then began his journey, after four days of riding he came to a deep dark forest. He was about halfway through the forest when he saw thieves but they did not see him. Quickly he went to a magic puddle, took off the diamond of light held it by the string and dipped it in and when he pulled it out all the bits that had touched the puddle had disappeared. Suddenly he saw the thieves behind him they were 100 metres away.

He ran to the cart and rode to the magic time puddle and when the horses touched it they, him and the cart with them completely disappeared. The next thing Valiant knew he was in an Aztec village.

press space bar to continue

**Figure 1.2** Ben aged 10 years 2 weeks. Free writing making up a plot for a computer game, Ben's passion at the time. He had asked for the spelling of several words.

## Dyslexia and development

The cognitive impairments or differences that underlie dyslexia persist into adulthood although in well-remediated or milder cases these might only show up under particularly testing or time-constrained conditions. How dyslexia manifests itself depends on the age of the child and the environmental demands that are being made.

## Indicators at pre-school level

- Family history of literacy difficulties;
- delayed spoken language and/or early speech and language intervention;
- difficulty learning nursery rhymes;
- difficulty with verbal sequencing e.g. alphabet, days of the week, etc.;
- poor gross motor coordination e.g. slow learning to ride a bike, swim, etc.;
- poor fine motor skills e.g. copying shapes or letters;
- shows little interest in identifying letters or words for fun;
- poor short-term memory skills e.g. remembering names, instructions.

## Primary age

### Reading

- Poor rhyme and alliteration detection;
- poor single word reading;
- reading hesitant and effortful;
- high number of reading errors for age;
- fails to recognise high-frequency words;
- reverses some words e.g. was and saw;
- fails to recognise word they have just recently read;
- misses out words or lines or reads some words or lines twice;
- listening comprehension better than reading comprehension;
- comprehension relatively better than speed and/or accuracy;
- difficulty maintaining place when reading;
- avoids reading/dislikes reading out loud (but enjoys listening to stories etc.);
- misreads sentences or instructions;
- confuses similar sounding words e.g. our, are;
- reading age below chronological age for fluency and accuracy.

Research indicates that children who enter education with poor letter knowledge and poor rhyme detection are at increased risk of reading difficulties.

## Spelling

- Avoids words they cannot spell, so written vocabulary appears limited;
- spelling age below chronological age;
- spells the same word several different ways in a passage of writing;
- forgets how to spell words learnt successfully for spelling test;
- several attempts to spell a word correctly with crossings out;
- spelling phonetic but incorrect e.g. frend for friend;
- leaves out a syllable e.g. sudly for suddenly;
- leaves out part of sound blend e.g. tet for tent;
- word spelt correctly but has wrong meaning e.g. their for there;
- correct letters but in wrong order e.g. organe for orange;
- incorrect or absent endings or suffixes e.g. run for running;
- mistaken word boundaries e.g. alot for a lot;
- letters reversed or mirrored e.g. bab for dad;
- letters may be close in sound to correct ones e.g. our for are.

Some words may be spelt bizarrely whereas with other words a phonetic attempt has been made. A number of the errors made are seen quite commonly in younger children but start to disappear from about the age of 7. With dyslexic children many of these errors persist for much longer. The type of errors made varies considerably among dyslexic children, with some children having a characteristic pattern of errors. The particular phonological skills, form of intervention and coping strategies that a child has will all influence the kind of errors they make. Several screening tests have been developed to try and detect children at risk of reading difficulties before they have started to fail in the classroom (see Chapter 2).

## Writing

- Poor letter formation;
- omits words and word endings;
- words crossed out;

- chaotic or messy layout of work;
- slow writing speed;
- limited amount of written output;
- mixture of upper and lower case letters;
- no or little punctuation e.g. capitals not used;
- reverses numbers, letters or words;
- difficulty copying from the board;
- difficulty with dictation.

## Numbers

- Difficulty learning multiplication tables;
- difficulty learning number facts;
- difficulty learning what operation a symbol signifies;
- poor mental arithmetic;
- difficulty reading number problems;
- difficulty arranging number work on the page;
- confuses direction of operation;
- reverses single numbers e.g. P for 9;
- reverses two digits e.g. 47 for 74.

Some of the number difficulties that dyslexic children have are related to their poor short-term memories. This gives them particular difficulty with mental arithmetic and the learning of number facts such as multiplication tables. In a sense they can be doubly disabled when carrying out mental arithmetic because as well as a poor short-term memory they have fewer number facts to call on to help them with their calculation. It is important to distinguish between *mental arithmetic* and *mathematics*.

Dyslexic children can have strong conceptual abilities and a good understanding of mathematics and for a proportion of dyslexic children this can be an area of the curriculum where they perform well.

## Other problems

- Dyslexia accompanied by other difficulties e.g. dyspraxia, ADHD;
- poor gross motor skills;
- poor organisational skills e.g. frequently loses pencils, items of clothing;
- poor memory leads to disorientation, cannot remember what day it is;
- confuses left and right;

- forgets instructions especially when part of a sequence;
- fatigue due to effort required to keep up with reading/writing.

Some researchers see dyslexia as part of a range of language and attention difficulties. Within this spectrum there are some children who have overlapping difficulties.

A degree of motor coordination difficulties is seen in a high percentage of dyslexic children and difficulties with hand-writing are particularly prominent. It has been observed that by Year 3 (7–8 years) children in primary school spend a third of their time on written activities (Alexander 1992). Some of these activities also involve reading written materials or instructions. So for a dyslexic child with poor reading, spelling, punctuation and handwriting skills a great deal of effort is required to try and complete these written activities.

## Possible secondary difficulties

- Self-esteem is lowered;
- child becomes withdrawn and subdued or difficult and disruptive;
- child is anxious when faced with literacy tasks;
- child dreads spelling tests;
- child dreads being asked to read out loud in front of classmates;
- child is inattentive;
- child avoids literacy tasks whenever possible;
- child lacks motivation;
- child thinks they are 'stupid' compared to other children in the class;
- child becomes socially isolated;
- child is teased because of literacy difficulties;
- child displays psychosomatic problems e.g. headaches, sickness.

With better early years screening, and systematic monitoring through the Literacy Hour, children with literacy difficulties should be increasingly identified and supported. Where screening is not high quality or children slip through the net it may be their behaviour which first draws the teacher's attention. At present there is debate about whether some children start out with a combination of literacy and attention problems or whether one problem is primary but leads to a secondary problem. What is clear is that there is a distinct group of children where dyslexia is the primary problem and behaviour, attention and motivation problems are a secondary consequence.

## *Identifying features in secondary school*

Many of the identifying features in secondary school will overlap with those listed for primary school. The features listed here are an extension of primary school difficulties and suggest those that are most salient or critical in the secondary setting.

### Written work

- Written work of lower standard than oral ability i.e. good comprehension and ideas not reflected in standard of written work;
- written work may show limited vocabulary compared to oral work;
- slow handwriting speed and/or poor legibility;
- poor note taking, especially when copying from board;
- written work has errors of punctuation and spelling but relatively good content;
- messy or chaotically set out work;
- work required under time constraints particularly affected e.g. dictation, rapid copying from board, written exercise in limited time;
- difficulty in copying down homework or assignment details at speed;
- difficulty recording competently carried out practicals in a written form;
- word-processed work of a far higher standard than handwritten work;
- does far better in tests or tasks with reduced writing requirements e.g. multiple choice questions or worksheets.

### Reading

- Reading age below chronological age and/or hesitant and laboured;
- reading comprehension may be compromised by effort required and lack of accuracy and fluency;
- reading is effortful and tiring so little sustained reading carried out;
- sometimes misreads questions or instructions;
- dislikes reading out loud in class;
- difficulty looking up words in dictionaries, etc.

## Other indicators

- Poor organisational skills e.g. forgets or confuses when homework should be handed in, difficulty following timetable, forgets equipment needed;
- mental arithmetic notably poorer than other aspects of mathematics;
- avoids literacy tasks whenever possible;
- frustrated or demoralised by poor literacy skills;
- low self-esteem for academic work;
- disruptive or withdrawn, may truant if pressures are too great;
- may develop positive or negative coping strategies (negative hiding reading difficulties, positive asking for help in reading texts).

In secondary schools the increasing need to perform tasks under time constraints and take responsibility for organising yourself come to the fore. Riddick (1996) found when she interviewed dyslexic children about their transition to the secondary school that the need to write at speed was of particular concern:

> *Like copying off the board, I get frustrated cause it slows us (me) down. Like the teacher will be speeding ahead and my writing's slow.* (David, 12 years)

> *If a teacher dictates work I can't write fast and neatly.* (Luke, 13 years)

> *It's difficult to get things down fast enough.* (Kathy, 12 years)
> (Riddick 1996: 123)

For dyslexic children of any age an important issue is the amount of effort required to keep up with literacy tasks and the fatigue and exhaustion this can lead to. Sophie (16 years), who often stayed up till midnight to complete her homework, made the following comment:

> *Everything, I think is hard going. I'm so wrecked. Tired after the day and just worn out by the effort.*

The transition to secondary school can, for some children, be a positive move. Children who have mild to moderate dyslexia and have been well remediated and supported in the past and have appropriate ongoing support and good coping strategies may well flourish at secondary school. Children who enter secondary school with literacy levels well below those required to access the curriculum, and poor ongoing support, motivation and coping strategies are more likely to flounder. A report by OFSTED (1999) which surveyed school practice noted that success in secondary school was linked to dyslexic children being identified and given appropriate support in primary school. This support needed to be highly structured and often involved multi-sensory approaches.

## Intervention

Some general issues related to intervention will be discussed here but more specific information will be given in the age-relevant chapters.

There are five basic components to supporting dyslexic children:

1. Direct help with specific difficulties to improve basic skills.
2. Improving curriculum access.
3. Encouraging effective and positive coping strategies.
4. Maintaining or improving self-esteem or confidence.
5. Creating an inclusive and dyslexia friendly environment.

In reality these components overlap considerably, but it is useful to consider them separately because the balance between them is important both at a whole-school and an individual class teaching level. There were concerns in the past about the remedial or withdrawal model because although children's specific skills were improved, this wasn't necessarily carried through effectively into the regular classroom. Mainstream teachers were not given help or support in improving curriculum access and creating an inclusive and dyslexia friendly environment. Dyslexic children were often misunderstood or misidentified and were in danger of developing low self-esteem and negative coping strategies. Alternatively some schools focused on trying to raise children's self-esteem and curriculum access but offered no direct help with specific literacy difficulties. Where children experienced no improvement in their basic literacy skills they were still in danger of struggling to keep up in the classroom and developing low self-esteem.

The balance between improving specific skills and developing strategies or organisation that allow the child to circumvent their difficulties is an important one to consider.

Present support strategies favour the use of within-class support for children with a range of learning difficulties. Critics have raised concerns that exclusive use of this approach had been to the detriment of specific literacy teaching (Moss and Reason 1998). Swanson (1999) carried out an overview of all the studies on interventions for children with reading disabilities and concluded that the following instructional principles underpinned successful forms of intervention:

*Direct help with specific difficulties to improve basic skills*

- specific instruction in phonemic decoding strategies;
- high intensity instruction;
- appropriate strategies for reading single words or text are systematically cued;
- plentiful opportunities for guided practice of new skills.

A critical factor for children with severe reading disabilities is that because they read less than other children they have considerably less practice at reading. A study by Cunningham and Stanovich (1998) compared the amount of reading out of school of fifth grade good readers (90th centile) and poor readers (10th centile). They estimated that a good reader might read in two days as many words as a poor reader would manage in a whole year outside of school. Some, but not all, poor readers may come from families where there is a history of literacy difficulties so that early programmes involving family literacy are important for some children. Torgesen (2001) has concluded from extensive research on reading intervention that because of the enormous deficits in reading practice that accompany reading disabilities it is imperative to have as much preventative intervention as possible in place. He maintains that the most critical factor in reading fluency is identification of single words and that by keeping such children's basic word reading skills within the normal range they will be able to read independently and accurately:

> If they can read independently and accurately, and they are also taught to enjoy reading, it is likely that they will experience roughly normal rates of growth in their sight vocabularies and thus be able to maintain more nearly average rates of reading fluency as they progress through the elementary school years. (Torgesen 2001: 199)

## The National Literacy Strategy

The National Literacy Strategy has been in operation in all primary schools in England and Wales since 1998. This involves teaching children a dedicated hour of systematic structured literacy skills including phonological awareness on a daily basis. Although the overall outcomes have been positive there have been concerns over a sub-group of children who have not made the expected progress within the structured framework of the Literacy Hour. It was argued that for these children the Literacy Hour was not sufficiently structured or sequential. In an attempt to remedy this Additional Literacy Support Materials for use at Key Stage 2 were developed and a video on progression in phonics was produced. This additional planning and support was helpful for some children but still was not meeting the needs of other children with severe literacy difficulties including those with dyslexia.

It was recognised that even earlier intervention was necessary in order to prevent some children from 'failing' in the Literacy Hour so in 2001 the Early Literacy Support Programme (ELSP) was introduced to reception classes, nurseries and playgroups. In addition, in the first term of Year 1, children who are not making progress in the Literacy Hour will be identified and in term 2 given daily planned support by a teaching or learning support assistant in addition to the normal Literacy Hour teaching. Individual or group support will continue in term 3 if necessary. In the pilot it was found that this additional support was best delivered in a quiet area away from the class but with clear teaching guidance for the teaching assistant.

Some schools use a mixture of within-class support and withdrawal for specialist teaching. A secondary school in Hartlepool for example runs a targeted literacy and keyboard programme for groups of selected Year 7, 8 and 9 children with specific literacy difficulties. This takes place during times like assembly so children are not missing out on key curriculum areas. Nottingham Dyslexia Association in collaboration with the City Council supports 15–16-year-old students from inner-city schools in attending a Touch-type, Read and Spell (TTRS) computer course. This is run at a Lifelong Learning Centre but is part of the schools' overall literacy support plans. Courses such as these, when part of an overall plan, both improve basic literacy skills and give children the skills required to improve their curriculum access and work output.

## Improving curriculum access

- Improving basic literacy skills;
- minimising the need for notetaking or providing support for notetaking (photocopied notes, laptop, scribe, etc.);
- worksheets, etc. appropriate for child's reading age;
- provide opportunities for child to contribute orally;
- support for recording homework or homework in pre-written form;

- peer or teaching assistant support for reading questions, instructions, etc.;
- technological support e.g. laptop computer, Dictaphone.

A major difficulty for dyslexic children is gaining access to the curriculum, especially where time constraints are to the fore. A Year 6 teacher noticed that a dyslexic boy in her class performed far better in mathematics when given a worksheet to fill in as opposed to copying from the board. When she observed him more closely she realised that he had great difficulty copying sums from the board and often spent the whole of the allotted time trying to do this.

How curriculum access is arranged will depend on the age of the child and the subject area being taught. Some forms of access can be arranged in an unobtrusive manner, for example, a group discussion involving filling in missing words on a worksheet, in a Year 9 history lesson. Other forms of support for accessing the curriculum are inherently more obtrusive, such as being the only child in the classroom with a laptop computer. The individual personality of the child and the ethos and practice of the particular school will influence how willing or unwilling an individual child is to receive more obtrusive forms of support. This is usually negotiated through the child's IEP on an individual basis as there is considerable variation in what children find acceptable:

> *Having the laptop was cool, it helped us (me) a lot.* (Louise, Year 10)

> *No way, not in front of my mates (talking about using a laptop in class).* (Callum, Year 10)

As well as access to the curriculum a critical point is how dyslexic children can output or effectively demonstrate their thinking and learning:

> *In my last school you would think of something and then you would just write down bits of it because you know it would be too hard to write all of it but when you've got a Dictaphone you can just say the full thing and it's just as easy as talking to someone.* (Carl, 14 years)

## Encouraging effective and positive coping strategies

All children have to adopt coping strategies to see their way through school, but where a child has a noticeable difference or difficulty they are often forced to develop more elaborate and far-reaching coping strategies. Coping strategies are sometimes divided into positive and negative strategies.

| Positive strategies | Negative strategies |
|---|---|
| Asking for help | Hiding a difficulty |
| Spending extra time on literacy tasks | Avoiding literacy tasks |

*Carl (14 years)*: I put down what I think, even if I don't know how to spell I still have a go, if I know I can't spell it I'll just ask someone next to me or something.

*Interviewer*: So you would ask other people?

*Carl*: Yes, but that is another problem though because I will turn around to ask someone a question and the teacher will shout at me or something. I get angry with the teachers when they do that though . . .

Because that is basically mean and it's like making you go down instead of up.

This underlines the importance of being aware of the kind of coping strategies a child is using and negotiating constructively over their effectiveness and appropriateness.

## *Maintaining or improving self-esteem or confidence*

There is both qualitative and quantitative evidence that children with dyslexia tend as a group to have lower self-esteem than other children. Closely linked to self-esteem is the idea of self-efficacy, in other words, how far you expect to succeed at a given task such as a spelling test or a comprehension exercise. Where individuals have high self-efficacy they tend to display more effort and persistence whereas individuals who do not expect to succeed give up more easily and invest less effort in the task. In terms of personal well-being and motivation to learn it is therefore vital to raise dyslexic children's self-esteem and self-efficacy. Strategies for doing this are discussed in Chapter 5.

## *Creating an inclusive and dyslexia friendly environment*

### Dyslexia friendly schools

As part of a move towards more inclusive educational policies the idea of dyslexia friendly schools has gained ground. 'The power of the concept seems to lie in the fact that changes made to become more dyslexia friendly also enable schools to become more effective' (Mackay 2001).

Many of the suggested changes for making a school dyslexia friendly will benefit the majority of children in the school.

Teaching study skills or keyboard skills for example will improve the learning of children in general and not just those with dyslexia.

Swansea LEA has led the way in developing a comprehensive dyslexia friendly schools' policy which involves (Springett 2002):

- dyslexia awareness training for all teachers and school governors;
- a specialist dyslexia-trained teacher in every school with accredited training for learning support assistants;
- early identification and intervention;
- higher level reading, language and study skills being taught;
- ICT support available when required;
- listening to children and liaising with parents being central to the policy;
- a resource bank of suitable materials to be available.

Swansea LEA reports that over the past four years the proportion of children statemented for dyslexia has dropped from 14 per cent to 2 per cent and that parents are now much happier with the level of dyslexia support provided by mainstream schools. Evidence in support of this is that an SEN tribunal on dyslexia has not taken place for two years and the local Dyslexia Association has reported a 50 per cent reduction in calls to their parent helpline since the policy has been put into practice.

A key part of this policy was allocating dyslexic children to the set that matched their intellectual ability rather than their literacy skills. Ben, the boy mentioned earlier in this chapter, first attended a secondary school where he was put in a bottom English set on the basis of his reading and spelling performance rather than his far better comprehension and analytic skills. The only support available was within class, which did not give him the intensive structured teaching that he needed. In Year 9 he moved to a school where he was put in a set for English that matched his intellectual abilities, was given intensive small group literacy teaching and had an English teacher who believed he could do well, and as a consequence he did.

The British Dyslexia Association (BDA) has developed a Dyslexia Friendly Schools pack which draws on the Swansea LEA approach (British Dyslexia Association 2000).

## Dyslexia friendly teachers

The level and nature of support and organisation for teaching dyslexic children varies across schools and LEAs but within their particular situation all teachers can endeavour to create a dyslexia friendly classroom by doing the following:

- create a positive image of dyslexia;
- make it OK for children to be dyslexic;
- teach in a multi-sensory manner;
- put a child in a set or group matched to their intellectual rather than literacy ability;
- believe the child can succeed and have high expectations;
- mark written work for content and not presentation (or mark them separately);
- give constructive advice on written presentation (not 'be less messy' or 'you must be more careful', etc.);
- be familiar with the child's IEP (if secondary school, have an organised system for reminding self which children in a class/set have IEPs);
- consult the child about their targets and how they would like any classroom-based support delivered;
- enable access to and output from the curriculum (prepared notes, workbooks, videos, Information Communication Technology (ICT), etc.);
- through teaching approach and organisation reduce chances for visible public indicators of the child's difficulties (i.e. do not say 'Hands up who has finished');
- never ask a dyslexic child to read out loud without ascertaining in private if they are happy to do so;
- identify and appreciate the child's strengths or particular interests/expertise;
- ensure the child receives more positive than negative feedback and that they receive at least as much attention and positive feedback as other children in the class (e.g. is their work displayed as often as other children's?).

If you find it difficult to put yourself in the place of a dyslexic child try writing with your non-preferred hand during an important meeting or seminar or writing something such as a form that will be open to public scrutiny. Try and imagine what it must be like to be under that sort of pressure for the whole of the day, week and year!

In England a revised SEN Code of Practice (DfES 2001) has come into operation which also takes into account statutory duties introduced by the Special Needs and Disability Act 2001. An Individual Education Plan (IEP) remains central to how support is delivered under this revised Code of Practice. Where a child is not making progress, plans should be drawn up by the SENCO in collaboration with the class or subject teachers and the child and his or her parents. This is known as School Action. Two of the triggers for School Action specified in the code are of particular relevance to dyslexic children:

1. Shows signs of difficulty in developing literacy or mathematics skills that result in poor attainment in some areas.
2. Presents persistent emotional and/or behavioural difficulties, which are not ameliorated by the behaviour management techniques usually employed in the school.

If at the IEP review it is still found that the child is not making the expected progress, outside support services can be called in to give advice on a new IEP. This is termed School Action Plus.

An important feature of the Code of Practice is that this covers children in Early Years Education settings (3–5 years) and it recognises the need to identify children with specific difficulties such as dyslexia at this early age.

The Code of Practice emphasises the responsibility that class teachers have for implementing support plans. It also specifies that schools can claim additional funding and resources to implement support under School Action and School Action Plus.

The code states that: 'Children who demonstrate features of ... specific learning difficulties such as dyslexia or dyspraxia, require specific programmes to aid progress in cognition and learning' (p. 86).

## Special Educational Needs Code of Practice

There are still considerable variations in how dyslexia is identified in different LEAs and even in different schools within one LEA. Initial assessment can be carried out by experienced SENCOs or dyslexia teachers using a combination of the literacy data collected on all children within the school, within-class assessment and observation and any specialist screening tests. Children are most likely to be referred on to the school's educational psychologist if progress is not made with the aid of a school-designed IEP.

Ashton (2001), a practising educational psychologist,

## Assessment

comments on the diversity of views and practices among educational psychologists in relation to identifying and assessing dyslexia and the tendency for some educational psychologists to have very strong and particular views. It is therefore difficult to generalise about the kind of assessment they will carry out but it should include some combination of standardised testing and in-context assessment. To some extent the way in which dyslexia is assessed will depend on the model of dyslexia that is being subscribed to. If the fairly narrow single word reading definition given by the BPS is used, assessment will focus on single word reading and spelling and phonological awareness. If a wider view of the cognitive impairments underlying dyslexia is taken then something like the Dyslexia Screening Test which assesses a variety of motor, memory, sequencing and phonological skills is more likely to be used (see Chapter 2 for assessment in the early years).

There has been criticism of the discrepancy approach to identifying dyslexia, where a discrepancy between the child's general intellectual functioning and reading and spelling ages has been looked for. The argument is that this may prejudice the identification of less cognitively able children. Others (Ashton 2001) would argue that IQ testing has an important role to play in highlighting the abilities of many dyslexic children who are underestimated at school because of their weak literacy skills. It also helps schools in allocating dyslexic children to appropriate ability groups or sets and to have a clearer idea of what cognitive resources the child can use to overcome their difficulties.

## Variations in the nature and severity of dyslexia

There is still considerable debate about whether there are clearly identifiable sub-types within dyslexia or whether dyslexia should be seen as part of a wider spectrum of specific learning difficulties. It remains uncertain how the core deficits in dyslexia interact with experience, specific forms of intervention and the child's wider cognitive abilities and preferred learning style and coping strategies. Where children have had a full psychological assessment some indication of severity may be given.

# Chapter 2

# Dyslexia in the Early Years

A range of research makes it clear that children have the cognitive deficits underlying dyslexia from their first years. In consequence there has been increasing interest in developing effective ways of identifying and supporting children at risk. Caution has to be exercised because of the variable way in which young children develop, so the aim at the pre-formal schooling level would be to identify children who are 'at risk' of developing reading and spelling problems. A diverse range of early years settings which are government-funded are required to 'have regard for the Code of Practice' (DfES 2001).

Current early years targets for literacy and pre-literacy skills provide opportunities for identifying children at an early age who are at risk of literacy difficulties but at the same time also expose some children to early failure if their difficulties in reaching these early targets are not understood. The code suggests that ongoing monitoring of children's progression through the foundation stages is essential and that a graduated approach to support should be taken.

A combination of the following factors would suggest that a child should be carefully monitored and supported if necessary:

- early speech and language delay;
- a family history of reading and spelling difficulties;
- difficulty learning the alphabet, days of the week, etc.;
- slower relative to other children in fine motor skills (e.g. doing up buttons, zips, shoelaces);
- enjoys listening to stories but avoids early literacy practice;
- difficulty learning nursery rhymes or detecting words that rhyme.

It is important to talk to parents if there are concerns. Taking a family history and asking tactfully about any of the above features is very helpful in putting together a fuller picture.

> **Case study: Mother of 6-year-old Kylie**
> *Well, looking back on it she was the last in our group (mother and baby group) to learn to speak, although she understood all right. She loved listening to stories but she never had any interest in nursery rhymes, she never recited them. She used to do her alphabet plaques by matching the shapes of the puzzle pieces; she never matched the letter and the picture. At nursery they said she avoided the drawing and writing table, never went near it, which I was surprised about because she had good concentration at home – she wasn't a restless child. She was a really happy toddler interested in everything, she used to have the whole bus in stitches asking me questions. When she started school I did wonder she still couldn't count to ten or say her alphabet, no idea about days of the week! But I noticed she became very quiet and subdued and started having terrible tantrums when she came home from school. She'd not done that before; even when she was a toddler she'd been incredibly easy.*
>
> *She loved being read stories but she'd no idea when we did that paired reading – she'd guess at anything. My brother can't spell either, he left school as soon as he could. One other thing I noticed was I could never teach her to tie her shoelaces, we tried all sorts of ways.*
>
> *She changed from being a carefree happy little girl into a tense tearful child, I just didn't know what was wrong to start with.*

Parents often report difficulties as soon as their children are introduced to formal literacy teaching with negative changes in their child's behaviour. Talking to parents is therefore an important part of early years identification and support.

## Screening and assessment in early years

In 2001 Durham LEA created a policy and guidance document for specific learning difficulties. In it they specify the sources and type of information that may be used to identify a child as 'at risk' or having specific learning difficulties:

- from other early years professionals (especially speech and language therapists);
- from parents or carers.

Nursery or school-based assessment may include:

- baseline assessment;
- National Curriculum attainment targets;
- checklists;
- standardised tests;
- diagnostic assessment measures;
- ongoing curriculum assessment.

Durham LEA concludes that 'Whatever information is used the essential prerequisite for Specific Learning Difficulties to be evident is the differential performance across the pupil profile of attainment and skills.'

Because some children with speech and language difficulties have a higher risk of dyslexia this will be an important area of liaison, especially in the early years when they will also have been supported by speech and language services. As well as standardised tests of reading, spelling and ability, there are also tests designed to look at specific phonological and short-term memory difficulties. These include:

*The Graded Non-word Reading Test* (Snowling *et al.* 1996);
*The Children's Test of Non-word Repetition* (Gathercole and Baddley 1996);
*Phonological Assessment Battery (PhAB)* (Frederickson *et al.* 1997).

Because dyslexia is a complex and multi-faceted syndrome, more comprehensive forms of screening and assessment which include a variety of sub-tests have been developed. These are found to be more sensitive and reliable than using single tests:

*Dyslexia Early Screening Test* (Nicolson and Fawcett 1996). Age 4.6–6.6 years. This has 11 sub-tests including ones focusing on phonological processing, motor skills, automaticity and memory.
*Pre-School Early Screening Tests* (Fawcett and Nicolson 2001). Age 3–5 years.
*Baseline Early Skills Tests* (Fawcett *et al.* 2000).
*Computerized Cognitive Profiling System* (Singleton 1997). This has nine sub-tests which are all carried out on the computer screen with the child's memory being tested for example by indicating on the screen which burrows the rabbit has visited.

These more comprehensive screening and assessment tests have been piloted with selected early years settings and are used regularly by some of them. Johnson, Peer and Lee (2001) cite the example of Middleton in Teesdale Primary and Nursery School where there is a three-stage assessment policy:

1. Initial profiling at three years on entry.
2. Continuous assessment between three and four years.
3. Skill screening/screening for dyslexia on child's fourth birthday.

Intervention based on the assessment is then planned.

Frith (1995) says that the following signs are usually seen in children identified as dyslexic:

- delayed speech acquisition and problems in early speech production;
- object naming and word retrieval difficulties;
- poor verbal short-term memory;
- difficulty in segmenting phonemes;
- poor at non-word repetition.

## Phonological skills

In recent years, there has been a lot of work undertaken into the acquisition of reading skills and, in particular, into links between reading and phonological skills. It is clear that children who have difficulties with language and especially phonological skills find it more difficult to acquire skills that are needed for both spelling and reading.

Lundberg and Hoien (2001), whose list of phonological difficulties was given in Chapter 1, observe that: 'people can have a marked deficiency in dealing with phonemes yet still have perfectly good cognitive abilities in all other areas'.

## Language and literacy development

In their early years training package, *Language and Literacy: Joining Together*, Wood *et al.* (2000) highlight the need to develop language skills with very young children as this leads, in part, to the development of phonological skills.

For most people, language skills and learning to talk is a natural process. For those with phonological difficulties it may appear that even trying to access their phonological skills is complex.

Snowling and Nation (1997) showed that children who start school with delayed speech and language skills have a poor foundation for literacy development. In addition the longitudinal study by Scarborough (1990) showed that those who had poor literacy skills at 7 years of age had been shown to have poor vocabulary at 3 years and poor naming and phonological skills at 5 years. Scarborough concluded that early difficulties with learning words might indicate later literacy difficulties. One of the key pieces of work in this area was undertaken in 1983 by Bradley and Bryant and showed that phonological awareness in pre-school children is a strong predictor of later literacy ability. Stanovich and Siegal (1994) and Byrne (1998) showed that children who were poor readers have poor phonological awareness skills but, given phono-logical awareness training, can make additional progress in reading development.

Law *et al.* (1998) indicated that up to 74 per cent of children with early speech and language delays have reading problems at the age of 8. If these are not resolved by 5 years of age, the child is at high risk of having language and literacy difficulties throughout their school years and into adolescence. Stackhouse (2000) showed that poor listening skills appear to be a precursor to early phonological awareness skills and lead to a delay in language development and thus the child is more likely to have literacy difficulties.

## Enhancing reading behaviour

Kosikenin *et al.* (2000) showed that children are more likely to have a positive attitude to literacy if they regularly see adults reading and writing for a range of purposes. Another study by Wade and Moore (1998) involved a project giving parents of 9-month-old children information on how to read together. The conclusion was that the children who are read to more regularly at home become better readers than a control group. It should be pointed out that many dyslexic children are read to regularly and some dyslexic children come from highly literate homes, which makes their poor literacy progress even more striking. The concern is for those children at risk who may be further disadvantaged by lack of exposure to literacy practices. Some will have parents who also have literacy difficulties, so these parents will need support and encouragement to help them support their children. Early community literacy projects are of great value as is planning and support with individual parents. Often it is possible to identify someone in the wider family who can regularly read or look at books with the child. A single parent mother with literacy difficulties in collaboration with the reception class teacher came up with the following solution:

*I knew Danny needed help with his reading, so he stops at my sister's for tea and does his reading with her.*

## Early phonological activities

As has been stated, phonological skills are very important so it is necessary, at as early an age as possible, to introduce activities that can lead to the developing of phonological awareness, such as the identification of non-speech sounds. It is generally thought that children acquire syllable knowledge before phoneme knowledge and so the activities should be sequenced in such a way as to reflect this.

## Identification of non-speech sounds

These activities would relate to a child being able to identify an animal by the noise it makes e.g. 'woof, woof', for a dog; 'moo' for a cow and 'tweet' for a bird. Everyday objects could also be included such as 'tick tock' for a clock and 'ding-a-ling' for a bell. Many of these could be recorded on tape and a game played with the child where they have to identify the sound either with or without a picture clue. Such tasks might include identifying words as units within sentences. This can involve missing out words, 'Sing a —— of sixpence', or getting children to repeat single words from a simple sentence, 'This is a taxi, or car, or lorry, or bus.'

## *Syllable identification*

Another key skill is identifying the number of syllables in a word. This can be done by encouraging the child to tap or clap out the number of syllables in a word which is familiar to them e.g. 'dog', 'cow', 'snake' all have one syllable, 'parrot', 'hamster', 'hedgehog' all have two syllables. 'Guinea pig', 'crocodile', 'butterfly' have three. Animals such as 'caterpillar' have four. This work can be undertaken with a number of different groups of words. Other tasks involving animals that are familiar to the children often make the work more enjoyable.

## Syllable blending

Another activity involving syllables is syllable blending, where a word is split into its syllables. The word is then spoken to the child in syllables with short gaps between each syllable and the child is asked to say the completed word e.g. 'Rab – bit', 'Spi – der', 'Oc – to – pus'. This could be done with household objects such as 'table', 'ta – ble', 'computer', 'com – pu – ter'.

## Syllable deletion

Another task involving syllables is syllable deletion. This initially can be undertaken with compound words such as 'football' where the adult would say to the pupil 'say football'. This provides the opportunity to see how the child articulates that particular word and corrections could be made if it was deemed appropriate. The adult would then say, 'Say it again but don't say foot' or 'Say it again but don't say ball.' Picture clues could be provided to allow a degree of support for the child. Here two words e.g. 'snow' and 'man' are illustrated and a flap of paper or card is stuck over the illustration. These could then be joined to a picture of a snowman and the child would have to say the word 'snowman' and say it again but without saying the part of the compound word that was covered. The adult could then lift the flap and the child could say the whole word again. Hulme *et al.* (1998) found that these skills in segmentation were a better predictor of literacy progress than rhyming skills.

## Rhyme awareness

Another key skill is rhyme awareness. This can be done on a nonsense basis where the children start repeating nonsense sets of words that rhyme e.g. 'sumpy, thumpy, clumpy, dumpy' or 'finkie, binkie, inkie, tinkie'. This activity can also be undertaken using real words such as 'chair, bear, hair, where', or 'shell, bell, smell, well, fell'.

An extension of this activity would be to identify one word that does not rhyme out of a list of three. It is important that the words have a different meaning as children often will try to make semantic links e.g. a child presented with 'key', 'tree' and 'door' may say that 'door' and 'key' rhyme because you open the door with a key or even that 'door' and 'tree' rhyme because a door can be made out of wood which comes from a tree.

It is also useful to ascertain that the child can hold the three words in their memory before tackling such an activity. If not they may need to be provided with picture cards as a stimulus to help them retain the information. For example one might present 'bat', 'cat', 'tin', and the child would have to identify 'tin'. Alternatively they could be presented with 'calm', 'pool', 'arm', the child identifying 'pool'. As the child becomes more competent, then similar sounding words could be introduced, for example 'mop', 'cop', 'sob', with 'sob' being selected or 'match', 'badge', 'catch', and the child would be expected to repeat 'badge' as the word that did not rhyme with the other two. These latter words are examples of words where unvoiced and voiced phonemes can cause confusion and need a more keenly developed sense of discrimination.

## Nursery rhymes and rhyming songs

Most early years practitioners will incorporate nursery rhymes into their daily routine and this links with rhyme awareness. It is important that children are exposed to nursery rhymes and action rhymes. This enables them to appreciate words as well as the sounds and patterns they make in a way they might not usually experience in speech. It also helps them to develop an appreciation of how words can be linked with music as well as the rhythm and metre of songs. It might also be possible to make up simple rhymes about activities that have happened to the child, or to someone else in the family that day, so bringing context to the work.

### Onset identification

Onset/rime tasks are useful activities to which young children can be exposed, for example presenting children with a set of pictures and asking them to point to the one that begins with the 's' sound, to develop a sense of the 'onset'.

In these circumstances it is important that the correct phoneme is pronounced. Adults may need some training themselves as often extra phonemes are added to the pure sound. Adults should know the difference between unvoiced and voiced phonemes. That 's' makes a 'ssssss' sound and not 'su'. A useful and simple way to determine the correct sound is to select a word with that phoneme at the end and listen to what it sounds like. In the case of 'a', 'b', 'c', 'd', it would be 'Abba' (vowels are easy), 'rib', 'duck' and 'had'.

Another game which can help in the identification of onsets is to find the mistake. For example in the nursery rhyme 'Twinkle, Twinkle Little Star' the word 'star' could be changed to 'jar' and the rhyme said as 'Twinkle, Twinkle Little Jar' or changing 'Hill' to ' Mill' the rhyme 'Jack and Jill' would become 'Jack and Jill Went up the Mill'. The child would have to identify the incorrect word and may even supply the correct one or say what was incorrect about the new word. Children themselves could be encouraged to make simple rhymes including an incorrect word but ensuring the words that were supplied still rhymed.

## *Alliteration*

Alliteration is the use of the same consonant or vowel at the beginning of each word or stressed syllable in a line of verse. A famous example is 'Round the rugged rocks, the ragged rascal ran'. Others could be made up and illustrated e.g. 'Four furry foxes frying fish on the fire', 'Six slithering snakes sleep silently'. Even asking the child to think of all the things they can that start with a 'P' is a good task. Including a category can narrow this and provide a more structured support for the child. For example, list food beginning with 'B' or objects in the house that start with 'M'. A way to help children think through this task is to introduce their own categorisation. So if they were asked to think of animals that begin with a 'K' sound they might first think of pets: 'Kitten', 'Canary', then move on to farm animals: 'Cow', 'Calf', then wild or zoo animals: 'Kangaroo', 'Koala' 'Camel'. Many of these activities are well described and resourced in Hilsdon *et al.* (2002). An extension to these types of activities is to link them to the onset/rime activity, which leads us into helping phonological skills at a phoneme level.

### Phoneme blending

Activities at this level would include phoneme blending, which is a similar activity to syllable blending. A child might be verbally given the phonemes 'p – i – g' and have to blend them into 'pig' or 'n – e – s – t' to blend into 'nest'.

Some find using a visual prompt a helpful aid. This might be a set of counters, which reminds the child of the number of phonemes. They may wish to move them around so that with the word 'pig', the first counter is removed, another counter is put in its place, and the child is told that it makes a 'w' sound (the word would then be 'wig'). The final counter might be removed and another one put in its place. The child is told that it is 'n' and so they now have to blend the word in front of them, which has changed from 'wig' to 'win'. The middle counter could then be removed and replaced with one where the child is told it is an 'e'; the child blends the phonemes to form the word 'when' from 'win'. It is clear that spelling is not important, as this is a phonological skill and the child is listening to the sounds in the word.

**Phoneme deletion**

A phoneme deletion task would involve giving the child a word and asking them to say the word, then to say it again without the first or last sound. This is a similar task to that outlined in the syllable deletion tasks. For example the child might be asked to say 'meat'. The child would repeat the word 'meat'. Then the adult would say, 'say it again without the "m" sound'. At this point the child would say the word 'eat'. A similar example using the same word would be to say 'meat' without the 't' sound, deleting the final phoneme. In this case the correct response would be 'me'. As the child becomes more skilled at this kind of task, they might be asked to delete the second or third phoneme in a word such as 'nest', which without the 's' becomes 'net' or 'sweat', which without the 'w' becomes 'set.'

*Spoonerisms*

The next sort of task might involve spoonerisms. This might be as simple as changing the first sound in the word so that 'wet' with an 's' in front becomes 'set'; 'boot' with an 'r' in front becomes 'root'. These tasks are similar to onset/rime tasks. However, the spoonerism task could be developed to take two words, transposing the initial sounds of both. In this instance 'David Beckham' would become 'Bavid Deckham', and 'Britney Spears' would become 'Spritney Beers'. It could also be done with a series of objects in the room: 'bookcase' becomes 'cookbase', 'teacup' becomes 'keytup'.

*Sight vocabulary*

Early language skills are very important. However, there comes a point where the child will want to learn to read and will realise that the marks in books are meaningful to adults and it is these marks or letters which convey the meaning and carry the story in a book. The child will then need to develop their own sight vocabulary.

There are a variety of sets of words that are published within those in the National Literacy Strategy. However, the 100 most frequently used words, which are found in all reading, and given in SNIPP Plus (Northumberland County Council 2002), is a very useful list to learn.

As stated, it has been shown that the first 12 words constitute 25 per cent of all reading and the first 32 words constitute 33 per cent of all reading. Recent research undertaken by Jonathan Solity for his Essex Early Reading Project has shown that it is still the case that these 100 words constitute approximately 50 per cent of all reading even in adult books.

This means that dyslexic children gain maximum benefit from their efforts if they master this set of words. There are a variety of ways in which these words could be taught. This may well depend on the child's strengths or difficulties.

## Letter sounds

Children also benefit from knowing pure phonemes but in particular, the sounds that each letter of the alphabet makes. This gives them a good grounding when they are starting to use word attack skills, as they will be able to identify the first letter sound or the first phoneme. It is quite important when teaching that it is not always assumed that each letter will make its sound and, therefore, letters can be blended together. This obviously works well for 'cat' but not for 'the'.

Work by Hatcher (1994) shows that students learn best when they are taught phonic skills and phonological skills that coincide with one another. It might then be useful to initially look at two-letter words that may, in turn, become rhymes. This would then naturally lead on to work that could be linked to onsets.

## Onset – rime

Activities have already been described for using onsets and rimes when phonological skills were discussed. To develop this as a phonic skill, the letter shapes themselves would need to be introduced. For example, a child could learn sounds such as 'am', 'an', 'at', 'if', 'it', 'in', 'on', 'up', 'is' and 'as' and then, coupled with their letter knowledge, could put a 'c' in front of 'up', an 'h' in front of 'is', a 't' in front of 'an' and so on to show the formation of words.

This work could be developed by examining word families or onset/rime groups so, for example, 'an' could lead to 'fan', 'ran', 'can', 'man', 'than' and words such as 'and' could be introduced by using the phoneme at the end of the two-letter word.

### Consonant–vowel–consonant words

Phonic skills would further develop through three-letter words, which are usually consonant–vowel–consonant words. This inevitably leads into words that have final consonant blends such as 'bend', 'hang', 'lamp', 'silk'. Words that have initial consonant blends such as 'blast', 'grip', 'plot', 'trim', 'crab' would also be taught.

## Digraphs

Initial consonant digraph words, where 'ch', 'sh', 'th', 'wh', blends come at the beginning of words such as 'chat', 'shot', 'thin', 'when', and when they come at the end such as 'much', 'push' and 'path', would be an appropriate next phase before moving into vowel digraphs where the two vowels are put together to make a different sound. For example the letters 'ea', 'oa', 'ee', 'oo', 'ai' are all used in words where they form a different sound. The split digraph or 'magic "E" rule', is generally considered to be a difficult rule for children to grasp, and so should not be dealt with too early. Following this would be words that contain silent letters; double consonants could be tackled. The progression would move on through very irregular words and perhaps subject-specific words as the pupil became older.

## Recording phonic progress

In all these progressions it is important to move at the speed of the child and not try to introduce concepts they are not ready for or move at a fast pace because it is perceived that the child should be at a particular stage because of their age. There are a number of schemes including ELS and ALS connected to the National Literacy Strategy that provide activities and strategies for each of these skills. A useful way of recording this is also found in SNIPP Plus (Northumberland County Council 2002).

## Teaching styles

There are numerous ways of delivering phonic skills in school. Teachers have a broad range of techniques available to them. What is clearly needed when teaching the dyslexic pupil is a range of strategies that match their learning style. For this reason it is very useful to scan through a variety of teaching books and make a note of different techniques. These can be held on a database as a back-up when teaching strategies with one method do not seem to be having as much effect as would have been hoped. Constantly asking oneself whether the child is receiving a variety of stimuli and whether this is addressing the child's dominant mode of leaning will usually bring positive results.

## *Spelling*

As a child's reading develops, so their spelling skills need to be taught alongside.

There are a number of ways of teaching spelling. However, interesting work undertaken by Brooks and Weeks for the DfEE (1999) indicates that children learn best when they are taught in a way that most suits their particular learning style. A summary of Brooks and Weeks' research can be found in the *Special Children Magazine* (2001). This work is expanded upon in Chapter 3 for the middle years.

SNIPP Plus outlines three checklists of spelling words that may be useful to work through and these lists can be taught using the methods outlined and recorded on the sheets provided.

## *Listening skills*

All these tasks, previously described, rely heavily on the listening skills of the pupil. It is clear that activities should be undertaken to try and help a child develop their listening skills and repeat back key words and phrases so that the adult has some way of assessing how much the child has grasped of the concept or skill which has been taught.

Reading is an interactive process and skills build up on one another, so the more skills a child can access, the more competent a reader they will become. For many children, acquiring these skills might happen almost as if by chance; they collect information from their environment and process it. However, usually for the dyslexic these skills have to be specifically learnt and so they need to be specifically taught.

### Matthew effect

Those children who lack competence in the reading skills or 'pre-reading skills' described in this chapter, tend to find reading difficult as they lack access to the skills that others may have acquired. Keith Stanovich (1986) described this as the 'Matthew effect'.

Many people think that the most effective way to acquire the skills needed to read is by reading. Continued reading practice promotes reading skills and is essential to develop the skills needed as a reader. As discussed earlier in the chapter it is important to put plans in place with parents and learning support assistants, etc. to ensure regular enjoyable reading practice. Even at this early stage some children are very sensitive to 'failure' on tasks they find difficult. As well as devising a well-structured intervention plan it is important to think about the social context in which this is delivered.

- Child needs to be given a positive message about any additional support;
- Child needs to be reassured that they are competent in many other skills;
- Child needs to be reassured they are competent at important aspects of literacy, e.g. listening to stories, thinking up ideas, asking questions, etc.;
- Parents can help reinforce these positive messages.

How young children react is very individual. Some seem quite happy or unaware of the implications of extra support whereas others can interpret it in ways quite unintended by adults.

*He thought it was a punishment (the small group support teaching), he thought he was a bad boy because he couldn't read, he said he was to blame and that's why he was being punished. I had to spend a lot of time telling him it wasn't his fault, that he wasn't to blame. That English was a really silly language and that lots of children have problems with the 'silly' bits and look at all the things he was good at.* (Mother of 6-year-old Nathan)

Phonological and early reading skills have been focused on because evidence to date suggests that this is the critical area to intervene in. But it should be borne in mind that a high proportion of dyslexic children also have some coordination and organisation difficulties. Other skills such as handwriting, holding a pen comfortably and performing a variety of motor tasks also need to be addressed. As commented on in Chapter 5 poor motor skills in combination with literacy difficulties can make the child particularly vulnerable to low self-esteem and teasing or exclusion by peers.

It is clear that formulating and utilising good individual education plans from the earliest stages is beneficial. There is a helpful unit in the SENAT materials published by Northumberland County Council on programme planning. Early intervention is crucial. Intervening when it may not have been necessary is more appropriate than waiting until later in the child's life before anything is done to help them gain literacy skills. Access to appropriate learning opportunities is vital and today teaching staff are under enormous pressure to keep the pace moving so as to cover the variety of strategies available. The positive message is that good-quality, well-targeted intensive teaching in the early years will lead to a more successful outcome than delaying it until later in the child's school career when a pattern of failure has been established.

*Chapter 3*

# Dyslexia in the Middle School Years

For children with literacy difficulties the middle school years are a critical time. Without appropriate teaching and support they have increasing difficulty in accessing the curriculum and become increasingly aware of the difference in their reading, writing and spelling performance compared to that of other children. Less access to written material can also disadvantage them in terms of ideas, enrichment, information, skill practice and sheer enjoyment of books.

*I'll never be able to do as good as other children.* (Liam, 8 years)

It is useful to check a child's learning and experiences at school against the framework for support suggested in Chapter 1:

- specific targeted teaching;
- curriculum access;
- maintaining self-esteem;
- developing positive coping strategies;
- dyslexia friendly classroom.

---

**Case study: Lindsay, 9 years**
*Her teacher had drawn up a planned programme of specific teaching of spelling which was delivered by the Learning Support Assistant. Her parents as part of the overall plan read with her every night for 10–15 minutes and then read to her for a further 15 minutes or more. This ensured she was practising reading material of an appropriate level of difficulty but also gaining access to more sophisticated texts that she found too difficult to read independently.*

---

*Her teacher used oral and group teaching methods and rarely required extended work to be copied from the board. She was allowed to work with supportive peers who would read out instructions, etc. The teacher or the LSA would also ensure she understood written materials. She was encouraged to use her full vocabulary when writing and not to avoid words she could not spell. She was sometimes allowed to use a Dictaphone or a word processor to record her ideas. This was part of the teacher's whole-class teaching approach so Lindsay did not feel singled out.*

*Lindsay was very keen on animals and helped at a city farm. Her knowledge and experience were drawn on and she gave a presentation with two friends and was also helped to make a poster for display. She was praised for the effort and ideas she put into written work and given constructive specific agreed targets to work on.*

*Lindsay was being taught how to use a Franklin spellchecker and also an ACE dictionary. Her teacher had talked to Lindsay and her parents about what things she found most difficult in the classroom. She had also encouraged Lindsay to list the strategies she could use when she was stuck. Lindsay was a sociable child who had good support from two friends so this was identified as a strength that could be worked with.*

*Her teacher used a number of teaching methods to suit different learning styles including multi-sensory methods.*

*Lindsay said that she generally enjoyed school although she felt 'fed up' when they had to do writing. She admitted that she still tended to avoid words she thought she could not spell. Her teacher and LSA were aware of this and were planning to work on strategies to encourage her to use a wider vocabulary. Both her parents and the school noted that Lindsay liked to get things right and was reluctant to risk failure. The previous year she had been criticised for her 'untidy' handwriting and as a consequence she now wrote microscopically small and very slowly and her work was therefore very difficult to read. The class teacher had been hoping to encourage her to increase the size of her handwriting but found that Lindsay became very anxious and upset when the subject was raised. It was decided to leave this for later in the year when hopefully her confidence would have increased. She already had a good relationship with the LSA so it was planned that she would use a graded approach with specific guides for Lindsay and gold stars for reaching the set targets for handwriting size.*

This particular case study brings up a number of issues that are common to many children with literacy difficulties.

There is often a discrepancy between their level of reading and their level of interest and comprehension. It is therefore important to find strategies for reading practice but also for accessing more sophisticated texts. Using adults or older children as readers is one solution as is the use of audiotapes.

Some dyslexic children become very sensitive to anything they perceive as criticism (Riddick 1996). Edwards (1994) noticed that 'oversensitivity to criticism' was one of the common features of the eight dyslexic boys she interviewed. One of the challenges for teachers is how to give constructive feedback to children who may have already encountered 'failure'. Hopefully involving children in setting targets for their IEPs and setting them up in a way that ensures a high success rate should help them to feel less criticised. Pollock and Waller (1994) suggest that children should never be directly criticised about their handwriting but should be invited to say how they would like to improve it. Sometimes more creative fun approaches can be useful with younger children. One teacher wrote with a glove puppet and got the child in question to give the puppet instructions on where to start letters and so on. She would make deliberate mistakes and do silly things that the child found very funny. He relaxed considerably and would show the puppet how to write a letter correctly.

Children quickly learn to adopt coping strategies to see them through the school day. Interviews with dyslexic children (Riddick 1996) revealed the following coping strategies:

- avoiding words they cannot spell;
- avoiding or putting off writing;
- writing less than other children;
- asking friends for help.

It was also apparent that some children spent a lot of time trying to hide their difficulties and were in constant fear of being 'found out'. Negative coping strategies such as avoiding writing or words they cannot spell appear to increase with age. It is therefore important to try and help children develop positive coping strategies such as using a spellchecker or asking a friend for the spelling of a word.

## Assessment

The Revised Code of Practice (2001) stresses looking at the rate of progress children are making. In the middle years it is important that students progress at a good rate in order to acquire the skills that they will need in later life. It is the role of the skilled teacher to ensure progress is maintained at an individual level. (Assessment strategies outlined in Chapter 2 are also relevant.)

Undertaking basic assessment work is very helpful. Even assessments such as examining hearing and vision regularly will provide important information which could avoid long-lasting detrimental effects occurring to literacy development.

It is very important to consider the pupils' views when looking at activities they enjoy or don't enjoy in school. Asking about what they find difficult and why they think they find it difficult can also be illuminating.

> *I hate it, really hate it, I'd do anything else rather than that (writing). I'm always last doing the boring stuff so I never get to do anything interesting, like the children that finish early they can do interesting things. I never get to do that.* (Kylie, 9 years)

Children often have quite specific views about the type of support from which they think they benefit most, what it feels like when they read and when they think they have greatest difficulty. Information like this can help avoid difficult situations arising in class, such as the student being asked to read out aloud in front of peers – a situation most dyslexic students find extremely embarrassing. Just as with younger children, it is helpful to check phonological difficulties. Informal assessments could be undertaken or more structured assessments like PhAB (Frederickson *et al.* 1997) could be used.

Assessment of the student's reading, in terms of single word tests and reading prose, can be helpful. Undertaking a miscue analysis of the book that the child is currently reading can do this or by using a standardised test if that is thought to be more helpful. Similar information should also be collected on spelling, asking the pupil to write for a limited period of time, perhaps five minutes, as well as using a more structured test of spelling, e.g. a Graded Word Spelling Test.

In both cases by comparing performance when context can be used and when words are presented in isolation, a broader picture of the student's abilities can be ascertained, leading to a more definitive programme being constructed.

Suitable checklists for both reading and spelling can be found in SNIPP Plus. As previously stated, an important part of assessment is the intervention which takes place following the identification of the strengths and difficulties. These should be tackled in a systematic way with a lot of repetition and over-learning.

Assessment, based on the skills and knowledge that the student has acquired at a specific time, can be helpful. Criteria reference tests often allow the prediction of targets for the next stage of teaching which can easily be translated into IEP targets. A simple example of this type of test would be a letter recognition or sight word assessment, whereby a new set of words could be targeted each time the previous set had been mastered. Regular teaching and assessing of progress allowing readjustment of the teaching programme is essential to discover if mastery has occurred, which, in turn, would lead to tackling the next specific target group of words.

## The whole system approach

Jonathan Solity (1996) wrote:

> When children fall behind their peers in learning literacy and numeracy skills, a discrepancy emerges between their actual and expected attainments, this discrepancy is invariably assumed to be the consequence of children experiencing difficulties in learning and results in a period of assessment to investigate the cause of the difficulty. A view that the failure to progress is the result of a learning difficulty is underpinned by a number of assumptions, perhaps the most significant being the assumption that the quality of teaching has been satisfactory and is not a causal factor in children's low achievement. (p. 46)

Solity has gone on to investigate the most effective ways of teaching children assumed to have learning difficulties, through classroom-based research. He focuses on providing the correct resources both for the student to learn and for the teacher to be able to deliver effective teaching.

His other focus is on the procedures that need to take place for the learning and teaching to be most efficient. Solity starts from a premise that all children can learn and reach age- and skill-appropriate targets in literacy and numeracy. This has been effectively demonstrated with the work he has undertaken in the Essex Early Reading Research Project, which is a joint collaborative project between the University of Warwick and Essex Local Education Authority. He has shown that, by undertaking a precision teaching-based assessment, teaching regularly for short periods of time and monitoring the effectiveness of this teaching, students can learn more effectively and teachers can teach more efficiently. This in turn allows the teacher to maximise the amount of time they spend with each student and to monitor the progress that is made.

### Precision teaching

This method provides a helpful way to implement the notion of 'noticing and adjusting'. As the charting is on a daily basis the student's progress can be monitored carefully. The times when the student is not learning can be quickly identified and adjustments can be made to the environment, the teaching technique, teaching procedure or the amount that is being asked of the student. This can also aid the effective production of Individual Education Plans (IEPs), as the work that needs to be undertaken on a precision teaching programme needs to start off with SMART targets, those which are specific, measurable, achievable, relevant and time-limited. The method also produces a very effective way of measuring accuracy and fluency as records are produced in terms of rate per minute.

## Fluency

There are other important skills to develop as well as accuracy: fluency and generalisation are also important skills. It may well be that any assessment undertaken needs to be structured in such a way as to measure the way in which these skills develop alongside one another.

## National Literacy Strategy

Now that a National Literacy Strategy is in place in most schools the teachers within them need to find a way of delivering this approach to all students. It is clear that for some pupils the pace is too fast and not rigorous enough as they find it difficult to consolidate the information they have learnt. However, there appear to be links between some of the techniques that would have been used for children who have special educational needs and some which have usually been thought of as being applicable for those who work with dyslexic students. These methodologies have been identified by the work undertaken by Pietrowski and Reason (2000). With adjustments, carefully monitoring what each child has learnt and how the skills and knowledge that they are acquiring can be consolidated, it seems that the National Literacy Strategy could provide the basis for the kinds of approaches recommended for children who have dyslexic difficulties.

## Teaching and learning styles

It is generally accepted that providing teaching in a variety of styles is the most effective way to develop students' learning. It is important to introduce visual, auditory, tactile as well as kinaesthetic ways of learning so that the student can see, hear, say, write, touch and move in order to learn. This will tend to improve the pathways to the brain and enhance learning. Teachers need to note which is the most effective style to use with their dyslexic pupil and be prepared to review and revise this depending on the task.

It is always useful to assess which is the pupil's strongest approach to learning although combining two, three or more different approaches will often strengthen the links for the pupil and enhance their learning.

Many teaching programmes for dyslexic children are based on the methods devised by Gillingham and Stillman (1956), who pioneered multi-sensory teaching in the 1930s and defined it in 1956 as being based upon the constant use of how a letter or word looks, how it sounds and how the speech organs or the hand and mouth feel when producing it.

Teaching pupils from an early age, using a variety of teaching styles, provides training and experiences allowing pupils to make conscious links between these inputs so that the best possible learning is achieved. A very helpful approach would be to encourage students to look carefully at letters and words, listen to the sounds that they make, then say the letters or words before writing or tracing them.

In his *Dyslexia: A Practitioner's Handbook* Gavin Reid gives an interesting overview of learning styles (1998: 134–41).

## Spelling

Brooks and Weeks (1999) undertook research which showed that by teaching spelling according to the individual's preferred learning style, gains of up to twice as much as would usually be expected could be made. In a summary article in *Special Children Magazine*, 'Spelling progress can be doubled', Brooks *et al.* (2001) describe their work for the DfEE in report RR108. They showed that by using individual learning strategies, dyslexic children's rates of learning to spell could be increased.

They targeted a variety of spelling strategies including Neurolinguistic Programming; Onset-rime; Look, cover, write, check; Own voice; Simultaneous oral spelling; Picture association; Mnemonics; Phonics and Look and Say. The children's teachers were asked to use different methods each week to teach spelling and asked to plot the progress over the week on a simple graph and then select the method where the rate of progress was steepest. The children were then encouraged to use their best method when learning any words. They found that in general 'children using their own learning methods approximately doubled the rate that they learned spellings compared with children who did not individualise their learning' (Brooks *et al.* 2001).

## Individual Education Plans

It is very important that the pupils themselves should be involved in the development of their IEPs even from an early age. They should know exactly what their targets entail as this should be a priority for the student as well as the adults who construct the IEP with the student. Personal involvement in monitoring their progress towards achieving success in the targets is also very important and can act as a strong motivational force. It is also important that the targets which are set are achievable within a relatively short space of time so that the student can see they are learning and thus enhance their own self-esteem.

It is important that IEPs don't include too many targets as this can become very difficult to monitor both from a student's and a teacher's point of view. Targets should be specific, e.g. is it clear to any visitor into the classroom what the student is being asked to do to achieve this particular target? IEP targets should also be measurable and make it possible to identify change by including quantifiable objectives. A target like 'the pupil will write six five-word sentences in five minutes' allows for simple alteration in the number of words per sentence.

Make targets attainable so the student has an opportunity to achieve their goal quickly and see their progress. It is also important to have a long-term target, and a medium-term goal but each pupil should have a very short-term target in which it is possible to gain success. Self-esteem can be a major inhibiting factor to many students and particularly to dyslexic students. Attaining targets helps raise self-esteem as the student has knowledge that they can progress and a measure of by how much they are improving. Regular monitoring of progress between the pupil and their mentor as well as the involvement of the pupils themselves in charting progress can also help.

Targets must be realistic. An account should be taken of the resources that are available to implement the teaching programme both in terms of human and material resources. Bearing in mind the student's preferred learning style this may involve a wide range of resources covering the auditory, visual, tactile and kinaesthetic. A feature of a good IEP target is that it is relevant to the student. Undertaking work that is in context and is meaningful is far better for the student as they can see a reason for the task and the dyslexic student will often take a novel approach to the task. Finally IEP targets should be time-limited, to be achieved within a certain timescale. This allows the pupil to know that this task will not be with them for ever.

When constructing IEPs it is always useful to identify what the student is currently doing. Target statements should be written in specific, positive terms and checklists to follow can be useful. Consider what the student should be able to achieve. It is helpful to think whether this behaviour can be observed and counted. Useful words to use are 'point to', 'name', 'match', 'copy', 'write', 'record onto tape'. Conversely, words such as 'know', 'remember', and 'develop the concept of' should be avoided. The next stage would be to consider the steps which are needed to achieve the target and to set targets in small achievable steps.

This would be followed by keeping a record of the progress under such headings as: date started, date achieved and date checked. This will entail including success criteria, so it is clear whether or not the target has been achieved, and then the date when checked. The targets should be reviewed regularly, so it is clear that progress has been maintained over time.

## *Numeracy*

Because of difficulties with short-term memory and rote learning dyslexic children often have difficulties in learning basic number facts and especially multiplication tables. Many of the dyslexic university students we have interviewed (Riddick *et al.* 1997) say that they still do not know their tables. For dyslexic children poor short-term memory means that their mental arithmetic performance is often weaker than their other number work. In addition problems with reading instructions, reversing numbers and the layout of their work can lead to errors (see Chapters 1 and 4 for further details). Despite this, many dyslexic children have good conceptual abilities and number work can be an area of strength for them:

- make sure they understand basic symbols: = + –, etc.;
- make sure they understand basic number language e.g. subtract, multiply, etc.;
- repeat learning and revision of number facts;
- teach child to estimate a sensible answer;
- teach child to check their answer against the set question;
- be alert for reversals which lead to child making a wrong calculation;
- practise counting forwards and backwards in sequences e.g. in ones then twos, etc.;
- use pattern methods to teach number bonds;
- teach multiplication using table squares;
- use squared paper to aid correct setting out of calculations;
- give a sample strip with digits in correct orientation for checking reversals;
- use multi-sensory teaching;
- rehearse what has just been learnt with oral revision at the end of the lesson;
- teach using logic rather than just rules so conceptual ability can be utilised.

The British Dyslexia Association has published a document entitled 'Dyslexia Friendly Schools'. Also many Local Education Authorities are following suit and producing their own guidance on creating Dyslexia Friendly Schools within their own boundaries. This coincides with the Revised Code of Practice which looks at meeting pupils' needs within the mainstream classroom, where possible, through a suitably differentiated curriculum but alongside intensive literacy training.

It is most helpful when all staff are aware of the difficulties faced by the students and can employ effective strategies to help develop their literacy and aid their access to the curriculum in a variety of subjects. To do this effectively schools will need to engage in a process which effectively tackles barriers to learning, maybe by using instruments such as the Index for Inclusion or strategies such as those advocated by the British Dyslexia Association in 'Dyslexia Friendly Schools'. It obviously helps when issues such as access to the curriculum for all are placed on the school development plan. This provides an incentive for the whole school community to tackle the issues and enables questions of budget to be investigated to support initiatives. It also allows governors the opportunity to look at the most efficient use of resources for all pupils within the school. This may involve buying new equipment or where possible employing new staff, for example a classroom assistant.

It is often the case that dyslexic pupils have low academic self-esteem (see Chapter 5). A whole-school approach can encourage valuing all skills, enable the creation of a school environment where everyone is valued and can encourage dyslexic pupils to display their skills, perform or discuss activities in which they are involved out of school.

One area of difficulty which faces schools is that while one or two members of staff may have attended a course in which good ideas were generated to create a Dyslexia Friendly School, that information needs to be disseminated, owned and taken on board by all. Some people may have knowledge of teaching styles or methods which may suit a number of children including dyslexic students but how can this be embraced by the whole school? One way is to have some whole-school INSET to look at ways of tackling these issues by all members of staff. This may also provide a springboard for other teachers to develop areas of specialist interest which could be a valuable resource in the future.

The inclusion of an area like this on the school development plan inevitably leads to the creating of a policy statement. As with all policies it is only useful if it is a working document. However, monitoring by the whole school community should ensure that it works. It needs to include expectations of change

## *Dyslexia Friendly Schools*

and a constant monitoring of progress towards the goal of access to the school environment for all.

Finally, opportunities to support the parents of dyslexic students need to be included in this type of approach (see Chapter 6).

## Solution-focused approach

An interesting approach to meeting the needs of pupils who are experiencing difficulties acquiring literacy skills is described by Rhodes and Ajmal (1995). In their book they look at using solution-focused approaches, made popular by Steve de Shazer, to work with pupils in schools. Solution-focused work usually encompasses a number of elements, the first of which is problem-free talk. This can be used at the beginning of the session with the student to develop a rapport and focus on the positive areas of their life. The session would move on to look at exceptions, for example, times when reading is easier. If an exception is suggested then a series of questions might follow, such as 'What is different about those times?' 'What do you do differently?' 'Who else is involved or notices these differences?' 'How could more of this happen?' 'How do you explain the differences?' 'How did you get that to happen?' (Rhodes and Ajmal 1995).

It is important that the pupil works at defining their own goals. For some this is a relatively straightforward procedure but for others they might only have a vague notion of what their goal is, for example 'I want to be able to read.' In such a case clarification questions will be needed, such as 'What will you be doing when you are able to read?' 'How will you know you can read?' 'What will be the first signs that you are starting to read?'

If this does not clarify goals then de Shazer (1994) suggested the use of scaled questions. This is where a scale from 1 to 10 is presented to the pupil and they are asked a question such as 'On this scale 1–10, where 1 is someone who cannot read at all and 10 is an excellent reader, where are you?' It is then easy to ask what they would be doing at the next point up. For example, if they rated themselves as 4 they might be asked the question 'What would you be doing when you were at 5?' This way they start setting achievable targets for themselves. The scaling question can be clarified by the use of a confidence rating scale. They would be asked 'On a scale 1–10, where 1 is you do not have any chance of achieving this and 10 is you are absolutely sure you can do it, where would you place yourself?' A score of 8, 9 or 10 would indicate a good chance of the student thinking they can achieve it. If it is lower they could look at what they set as a target and simplify it in order to make it more achievable. This is obviously best done in consultation with an adult.

In 1988 de Shazer claimed that often people have no vision of 'life without the problem'. With this in mind he designed the 'miracle question': 'Suppose that one night while you are asleep there is a miracle and this problem is solved. The miracle occurs while you are sleeping so you do not immediately know that it has occurred. When you wake up, what is the first thing you will notice that will let you know there has been a miracle?' 'What would be the first signs that the miracle had happened?' 'What would you find yourself doing that would be a sign of the miracle?' 'Who else would notice that the miracle had happened? How would you know they had noticed?' The ideas that emerge are elaborated on in as much detail as possible and the child is encouraged to describe the situation as they would like it to be. They now have a long-term goal to work towards.

The final part of the session would be paying compliments and setting tasks. Here the adult would compliment the student on something they said or an achievable goal they set and investigate a task to undertake before the next session.

Rhodes and Ajmal look at how this can be applied to pupils with literacy difficulties. They investigate the issue from the angle that many students with literacy difficulties have come to believe that they are unsuccessful learners. Many have been very active learners in other areas and most have even acquired some level of literacy skills. They argue that looking at exceptions can place some hesitation on their view that they cannot learn and supply confirmation of proficiency that can be built upon. They cite the sort of questions that could be asked: 'When did you make the most progress in learning to read?' 'What were you doing at these times which was helpful to you?' 'How did you know when you were making progress?' 'What helps you most at the moment?'

The solution-focused approach lends itself well to examining the metacognitive (thinking about learning) aspects of reading. Asking the right sort of questions allows the pupil to become more aware of the processes they are going through when they are approaching a reading task and more importantly what works for them. Rhodes and Ajmal suggest asking questions such as: 'How exactly do you learn to read and/or spell a word?' 'How do you learn to remember a word?' 'What is your best method of learning? What exactly do you do?' 'When you try to remember how to spell a word, what do you do? What are your thoughts?' 'Between now and the next time we meet, observe how you learn a word.'

They also address the motivational factors surrounding reading. If an adult is asked to engage in a task they dislike they often find a way of passing it to someone else or avoiding it. Unfortunately in school it is very difficult for students to avoid literacy skills even in a very differentiated curriculum.

Butkowsky and Willows (1980) showed that students who perceived themselves as poor readers had lower expectations of success, gave up when facing difficulties and if they did achieve any success, attributed it to chance. There are a number of dyslexic students who have reading motivational difficulties. Rhodes and Ajmal suggest asking questions such as: 'Do you want to learn to read? Are you sure? Why is that?' 'How much work are you willing to do? How much time will you spend reading in the evening?' 'On a scale 1–10 where 10 is I want to read enormously and 1 is I don't care at all, where would you place yourself?' 'What will be the first signs that you are making progress in reading?' 'When you can read, what will you read?' 'How will you know that you are a reader?' They also examine the beliefs of teachers who often find it difficult to keep motivation themselves with students who are making very slow progress. Solution-focused work would be highly advocated. If something has been tried for some time and it is found not to be working, then something different should be tried.

## Conclusion

It is clear that schools must undertake effective assessment for action to occur to help the student. This will lead to teachers constructing IEPs to meet the individual's needs, implementing them carefully and monitoring them closely to make sure that progress is being made. With School Action and School Action Plus, schools demonstrate that what they are providing is additional to and different from what most pupils in a mainstream school would experience.

It is clear that where a whole school takes action together, this situation can be made much easier for individual teachers as they will have resources beyond their classroom and the students will experience similar environments in whichever class they are taught. This whole-school approach to removing barriers to learning will help not only dyslexic pupils but all students who have difficulties in accessing the curriculum.

This approach is exemplified by Oldfield Primary School and is described here by the head teacher, Elizabeth Henderson.

**Case study: A dyslexia friendly school … almost by mistake!**

*Oldfield school has just been given Beacon status for writing and for being a dyslexia friendly school. This is a surprise to me as I have been at the school for only five years and had not set out to achieve the 'dyslexia friendly' status. It has grown out of a philosophy that genuinely tries to teach all the children in the school in a way in which they learn.*

Skilled Teaching

*All children have their own individual aptitudes and difficulties, which together create a need for some intelligence and adaptability on the part of their teachers. Dyslexic children are the largest group of pupils in each class with Special Educational Needs (SEN). Their needs must be identified and addressed as early as possible. Within all planning, for all lessons, good teachers have to be prepared to use multi-sensory methods, to make dreary 'over learning' enjoyable, to help memory with tricks of colour, imagery, impropriety and to watch and observe how the best learning takes place. The methods that are most effective for dyslexic pupils will also be best for most of the other children. Teachers need to be able to teach around a difficulty and methods that work for dyslexic children can be used for overcoming many other kinds of SEN problems. Watching how the child responds to our teaching and having a huge battery of ideas and methods to use, is the highest form of teaching skill and the one that will be most effective. Teachers' Assistants can frequently be very effective in finding alternative ways in which to approach a child's problem as they come from a 'common sense' base and are not cluttered with teachers' ideas and prejudices.*

Understanding Everywhere

*Everyone in the school, from Teachers to Caretakers and Dinner Controllers need to understand that children have different needs and that a good school understands them all and tries to cater for them all appropriately. We hold a termly meeting for the parents of children on the SEN register. Here they can discuss, informally with each other and the school's SENCO, any aspects of their children's education or development they are concerned about. Parents, siblings, grandparents, governors, volunteers and everyone else in the school learn to appreciate and value the children for themselves, for their individuality and for the richness they bring to the school. Dyslexic children are usually lucky as they often have aptitudes and skills that enrich many aspects of school life well.*

Opportunities to Shine

*It is these skills that allow the adults in a school to promote the self-esteem and confidence of dyslexic children, who are often in the winning teams in sports, are musical and love to perform, who act and present to an audience well or whose art is displayed and whose designs show originality.*

*At Oldfield we have special opportunities for the children to 'shine'. Each week children organise an amusement for the rest of the school; a quiz, a dance competition, a play or drama workshop, some conjuring tricks, a puppet show, a Yo-Yo display, skateboarding demonstration, a display of collections, etc. Any child of any age can offer to run these whole-school events, which are organised and run entirely without adult help.*

*Weekly 'music spots' allow pupils to perform on their instruments or sing to the school and at the end of term the children entertain each other at an end-of-term concert. These are the moments when teachers and friends see another side to some of the children in the school. These moments build respect from peers and increase self-confidence in the individuals concerned.*

## Success for Every Child
*Our clear objective is that every pupil can feel valued and be balanced and successful at school. Dyslexic children find so much of their academic work troublesome and hard; it is vital that they have rich experiences, many opportunities to succeed, a knowledge of their own abilities and a belief in themselves.*

*When school is over many dyslexic people make a success of their lives, but they must be given these chances early in their lives and their self-esteem must not have been damaged or their creativity squashed.*

*Elizabeth Henderson*

# Chapter 4

# Dyslexia at Secondary School

The period of transfer and adjustment to a new school is crucial to all pupils and may hold a particular challenge for a pupil with dyslexia.

Primary schools are required to transfer to secondary schools the school records for all pupils within 15 days of pupils ceasing to be registered at the previous school. The school should therefore be in possession of a good deal of useful information about the child, including detailed background information collated by the primary school SENCO and copies of IEPs. This information will undoubtedly help to shape curriculum and pastoral planning for the pupil in the first few months at secondary school.

If a close working relationship has been developed between the primary school and secondary school this will be beneficial for the child and assist planning. Informal discussion can highlight children's difficulties that may not be clearly visible in statistics.

The secondary school brings with it the advantage that students are taught by individual subject specialists who normally have a passion for that subject. If a dyslexic student has strengths in these areas then this can have a most positive effect on that individual's self-esteem. However, the organisation and movement in a secondary school may provide huge difficulties for the dyslexic student.

For statemented pupils, attending annual reviews by the secondary SENCO or representative in the final year of junior school can help the information gathering and sharing process. The annual review before transfer may be the first formal meeting between parents and a secondary school teacher. This meeting is vital in forming a good relationship and sound base to develop over the following five years of secondary schooling,

*Transfer to secondary school*

or seven if a sixth form is present at the school and the child wishes to continue education.

Additional assistance can be made by preparatory visits to the school prior to commencement of the school year. This decision is important depending on each individual case and each child's and family's wishes. Transfer to secondary school has been found to be a time of great anxiety for both child and parents.

Some of the information regarding individual needs may be obtained from:

- National Curriculum Levels.
- NFER Assessments.
- Standardised Tests.
- Educational Psychologist Assessment.
- Discussion with the primary school teacher.
- Discussion with parents.

The information can be supplemented by additional questions on the admission form asking parents for information about their child's needs. For example, does the child wear glasses? What help has the child received in the past? What help do they think their child will require? This involves parents in their child's education even before the child has begun secondary school and can help develop a working relationship between the school and family. This is useful as it begins to address parents' expectations of extra provision in the secondary school early in the child's attendance at secondary school rather than later when valuable time may have been lost.

The use of computer-assisted screening such as LASS (Lucid Assessment System for Schools) Secondary Computerised, multifunctional assessment has benefits for pupils 11–15 years 11 months of all abilities.

LASS Secondary has six broad applications:

1. Routine screening on entry to secondary education.
2. Screening of all students in the age range for literacy problems.
3. Assessment of special needs in literacy.
4. Identification of specific learning difficulties and dyslexia.
5. Regular monitoring of progress in literacy.
6. Assessment of general ability.

LASS Secondary is easy to administer: the computer delivers the assessment tasks to the pupils in the form of games, without the need for individual supervision, and scores the results immediately.

LASS Secondary comprises the following eight assessment modules that can be used individually or in combination:

1. Single word reading.
2. Sentence reading.
3. Spelling.
4. Reasoning.
5. Auditory memory ('mobile').
6. Visual memory ('cave').
7. Phonic skills ('non-words').
8. Phonological processing ('segments').

The full suite of eight computerised modules takes about 55 minutes on average to administer. Most of the modules are adaptive tests – that is, the computer automatically adjusts the difficulty of the items to suit the ability level of the pupil. This means that assessment is faster and more efficient and also prevents pupils becoming bored by items which are too easy, or frustrated by items that are too difficult. For each test instructions are spoken by the computer and practice items are given to familiarise the pupil with the test requirements. When the pupil has completed the practice items the test phase begins.

LASS Secondary enables teachers to:

- obtain a reasonable estimate of the pupil's intelligence;
- measure attainment and expected literacy attainment based on results;
- assess the pupil's attainment in reading and spelling and identify students who are underperforming in these areas;
- measure discrepancies between actual literacy attainment and expected literacy attainment based on intelligence;
- identify underlying problems in memory or phonological processing skills that could be the cause of under-performance in literacy;
- identify pupils with dyslexia (specific learning difficulty);
- monitor development in reading and spelling on a regular basis;
- assess improvements in memory, phonological and phonic decoding skills brought about by appropriate training or intervention.

The printing out of the profiles can be done during the night and collected by the SENCO the following morning to ensure confidentiality is maintained.

Dyslexia does not disappear and one does not grow out of it. A diagnosis is necessary and should not be regarded as a negative classification. If a child falls behind in learning to read and spell, it is advisable that the reason be investigated as soon as possible. It is only after a thorough assessment that informed planning can then address the issues to enable the student to access the curriculum. This assessment must be a continuous process to enable planning, delivery and review to become a cycle. Involved in this cycle are the student, parents, curriculum staff, pastoral staff, learning assistants or support teachers, special needs teachers and any other outside agencies which may be involved with a particular student. As the student becomes older their part in this planning and review can be of increasing importance. This allows the student to be a real part of the process.

It is essential to identify pupils with potential difficulties as soon as they enter the school. Several procedures are employed to identify pupils with learning difficulties:

- parents visiting the school before admission;
- liaison with junior school;
- Year 6 induction day, informal observations;
- Year 6 SEN transition observation and discussion of concerns raised by students;
- admission form completed by parents giving information as to any special educational needs, the graduated response the child is at on the SEN register as well as health concerns;
- primary school IEPs, statements, annual reviews, teachers' notes, discussion with head of year and SENCO;
- SAT results, test scores and teacher assessments;
- induction programme where teacher, pastoral staff and parents may highlight concerns;
- CAT scores;
- reading test score;
- spelling test score;
- LASS computer assessment providing information for visual and auditory memory, phonic decoding skills, phonological processing ability, spelling, reading and reasoning ability;
- SEN teacher observation checklist for observation and analysis of a piece of free writing, handwriting, spelling, etc.;
- effort and performance report grades across subjects with behaviour concerns highlighted;
- parents' evening review of the first term and parents and pupils involved in target setting;
- assessment made by qualified teacher in the Access and inclusion department.

These features can occur in dyslexic pupils across the ability range but are probably easier to identify initially in pupils of average or above general ability. They tire more quickly than a non-dyslexic person because far greater concentration is required. They may have difficulty with figures (e.g. learning tables), reading music or anything which entails interpreting symbols. Learning a foreign language is usually a problem. They may be inconsistent in performance, omit a word or words when writing, or write one twice. They may have constant nagging uncertainty about their performance and spend a great deal of energy on covering up their difficulties. Students with dyslexia often have difficulty taking adequate notes because they are unable to listen and write at the same time. Another potential problem is that when they look away from a book they are reading or the blackboard they are copying from, they may have great difficulty in finding their place again. They work more slowly because of their difficulties, so feel under constant time pressure.

*Characteristics of pupils with dyslexia*

> *Dan was told off for not using his ruler to underline headings during several geography lessons where he was required to copy notes from the board. He explained that he was under so much pressure to keep up that he did not dare to stop for a moment to rummage around in his bag to find his ruler, as he knew he would fall so far behind he would never catch up. When his writing speed was assessed it was found to be only nine words per minute; a speed far below that required to keep up with the speed of note taking in those lessons. (Dan, 14 years)*

Pupils may experience difficulties in:

- some or all aspects of written language including mathematics;
- organisation;
- short-term memory;
- fine motor skills;
- visual memory;
- auditory memory;
- sequencing;
- phonological awareness;
- confusion of left and right.

Each dyslexic child, while displaying some or all of the characteristics, will have a unique set of abilities and difficulties. These need to be recognised and they need to be taught appropriately. The success of such pupils in school has been found to depend on:

- early identification of their needs;
- full support of teachers and parents;

- constant boosts to self-esteem and motivation;
- peer group support.

## Children's perceptions

**A gifted boy in Year 11**

*Secondary school was difficult at first getting to know where everything is but then that was the same for everyone else. I have enjoyed secondary school because there are better facilities such as an art room, computers, science and PE.*

*Looking back the best thing that happened to me in secondary school was not doing a MFL (modern foreign language) and always having that time to work at my English and higher up the school it just gave me a breather and was helpful in keeping up with course work. One of the worst things that happened to me was when I had to go to extra reading, I missed out on an opportunity to take part in the Duke of Edinburgh Award Scheme I also missed out on other information. I also remember having to redo a piece of English work that had taken me hours to do but the teacher had no idea about this and looking at what everyone else had done made me redo it and add more to it.*

**A Year 10 girl**

*The best thing that I have done is having a good friend so when I forget things she can help me remember. It is little things that I forget and knowing that my friend can help takes the pressure off me. Extra time in examinations and school tests has helped me show what I know and developed my self-confidence.*

**A Year 9 girl**

*I found it very hard coming to secondary school because it was so big. I did not know many people and all the different teachers. I had just found out I was dyslexic and had not come to terms with it. I was very worried what other people would think of me. Now I feel OK about school and being dyslexic. The teachers have been understanding and I get lots of help – these things have made a difference for me.*

*My advice to other dyslexics is 'Do not let people put you down'; it does not matter what other people think it is how you feel inside. It is not an illness and I can do things other people find difficult. I am good at maths particularly shape and space, I am creative in art and DT.*

**A Year 8 boy**

*The best thing about being in secondary school is I have only three more years before I leave. The PE lessons are better I like going on the trampets.*

*I do not like extra help outside lessons and in lessons because it makes me different. I do not want to be different. I hate reading out loud in the classroom. I find I get too much homework teachers do not realise how long it takes me to do it. I like projects as I can spend a long time doing them on the computer by doing a little bit at a time.*

All these pupils were happy to discuss how they felt about secondary school and by gathering such information a lot can be learnt about how to deliver support both at an organisational level and at an individual level.

> **Case study**
> *A young man was referred to the SENCO by the Senior Learning Mentor, who was himself Dyslexic and Dyspraxic; a wonderful person to have in school who has a real understanding for the pupils and the problems they encounter. This young man in year 10 was impulsive, angry and getting into quite a number of confrontations with his teachers. He was found to have a reasoning centile of 87, very weak auditory and visual memory, an average reading score and first centile score for single word reading. He was unable to write down his thoughts as he said his brain worked too fast for his arm and hand when writing. His teachers have been informed about his difficulties and he is beginning to make progress.*

A number of dyslexics recall experiences similar to this and the words 'frustrated' and 'angry' are often used to describe how they felt. With better monitoring of reading, spelling, general reasoning and writing speed, students like this should be identified much earlier in their school career and given the support and understanding they need.

At present for a variety of reasons some children do slip through the net and class teachers should feel free to discuss any students they have concerns about.

## Role of SENCO

The SENCO, in collaboration with the head teacher and governing body, plays a key role in helping to determine the strategic development of the SEN policy and provision in the school to raise the achievement of pupils with SEN. The SENCO takes day-to-day responsibility for the operation of the SEN policy and coordination of the provision made for individual pupils with SEN, working closely with staff, parents, the Connexions PA and other agencies. The SENCO also provides related professional guidance to colleagues with the aim of securing high-quality teaching for pupils with SEN (Code of Practice 2001).

The SENCO has the responsibility to ensure students' legal rights are adhered to in respect of teaching and examination provision such as rest breaks, extra time, reader provision, etc. Be aware that a dyslexic may be undiagnosed as late as secondary school, and that compensatory strategies which the (un)diagnosed student evolved at the primary level may be inadequate for the more complex and multi-faceted secondary school curriculum.

## Learning support department

Schools have different systems to support children with learning difficulties including dyslexia. Some may have a department with a number of specialised teaching staff, teaching assistants and other helpers, others may just have one teacher. However, secondary schools may have increased flexibility in timetabling and specialist teacher knowledge.

The learning support department supports staff, individual pupils and parents in the following ways:

- Carrying out assessment and diagnostic procedures.
- Involving an Educational Psychologist or other outside agencies as necessary.
- Disseminating the results of assessment to staff.
- Ensuring that the requirements of the Code of Practice are followed.
- Maintaining the special needs register and a separate list of pupils diagnosed as having dyslexia.
- Writing IEPs for pupils; school action plus and statement, in conjunction with other staff, pupils and parents.
- Involving and supporting parents by being openly available at any time for discussion of concerns, by arranging reviews of progress and by mediating between parents and staff where concerns arise.
- Advising parents of voluntary organisations which can give independent advice and support.
- Arranging concessions in external examinations.
- Assisting in the provision of additional and modified resources.
- Arranging training for staff and departments as required.
- Disseminating information that might be useful as it becomes available.
- Providing individual programmes of work for pupils to use at home or school.
- Counselling pupils as necessary.
- Providing additional support to pupils and parents before and just after transfer from junior school, as required.

## Class teachers

Class teachers are important in the education of all children and have a particular responsibility to a dyslexic child as one word out of place can undo months of work by a specialist teacher.

*She's a nightmare, the Chemistry teacher. I hate going to her lessons. She really humiliates me, I dread it all day … I sometimes wish I could just leave school.*

Conversely class teachers who have a supportive approach can have a very positive influence on children's learning and well-being.

*My history teacher is really nice. She always encourages me. She never shouts even if I get something wrong. She's really helpful, she praises me. It does make me feel better, like somebody cares ... yes I do try harder.*

All teachers should ideally:

- Have a copy of the 'Access and Inclusion Register' or special needs register. This register gives a snapshot of a pupil's strengths and weaknesses. (It is also helpful for supply teachers to be given information about children they may meet.)
- Read all assessment and review reports available for individual pupils.
- Use the IEPs of pupils at School Action and School Action Plus in planning, delivery and assessment of lessons.
- Take every action possible to prevent teasing by other pupils.
- Use metacognitive techniques to ensure the pupil understands how he/she learns best and develop strategies that build on their learning style.
- Let the child know that their difficulties are understood.
- Discuss the details of the child's performance and achievement in terms of what they know about their difficulties.
- Refer to the school's Assessment Policy when correcting work and be as encouraging as possible.
- Ensure that the child can read written comments and corrections on work.
- Mark work for content separately from spelling, punctuation and presentation.
- Sit beside a pupil rather than opposite him/her when explaining tasks individually, to avoid directional confusion.
- Provide instruction in how to organise materials, essays, timetables, equipment, etc.
- As appropriate, teach the use of strategies such as mind-mapping and memory pegs.
- Provide taped versions of texts, tests and assessments, or a reader where possible, and allow extra time as necessary (access and inclusion staff can help with this).
- Encourage the use of word processors, spellcheckers and spelling dictionaries.
- Allow aids to note taking such as Dictaphones, photocopies of teachers' notes or a friend's notes, keyword and spelling lists.
- Check homework has been accurately recorded.
- Help to develop pupil's self-esteem.

- Allow more time for tasks such as getting out books, getting started, completing work. This includes practical tasks.

Above all, remain encouraging and positive. It can be difficult in a busy classroom to remember details of every child with special needs especially in schools with a large percentage of children on the special needs register. As a priority for dyslexic children note their:

- reading age (remember comprehension may be much better than fluency and accuracy);
- spelling age;
- writing speed.

Have some general principles of your own about how you respond to any child with a literacy difficulty in terms of issues like reading aloud, copying notes, etc.

## A cross-curricular strategy

A few ideas for using tape recorders/Dictaphones:

- with the permission of the teacher and/or under control of the teacher;
- use for recording wordy lessons when others are busy scribbling notes;
- use for group brainstorming sessions – easy to copy to other tapes for group members – makes SEN pupil very acceptable in a group;
- speak homework details;
- use to provide first draft for story/report and then transcribe to word processor;
- use to speak 'notes' from researching information from books;
- use to record actions/results in science/D&T/food technology;
- practical sessions;
- use as talking book support for maths textbooks;
- use as talking book support of other word-heavy subject textbooks;
- listen to talking books for pleasure;
- listen to their choice of music in leisure time to relax.

Teaching children through a combination of sensory experiences allows them to use their stronger or preferred learning style more effectively and to reinforce learning by linking auditory, visual, and kinaesthetic channels. Most people have a dominant learning style:

*Multi-sensory learning*

- *Auditory learners*: 20–30 per cent of school-age children remember what is heard. They remember by listening.
- *Kinaesthetic learners*: 30–40 per cent of school-age children remember when they use their hands or whole body to learn. They remember by doing.
- *Visual learners*: 40 per cent of school-age children remember what is seen. They remember by seeing.

## Addressing different learning styles in lessons

*Auditory learners:*
- Explain
- Repeat
- Discuss
- Use tapes
- Use poems
- Tell stories
- Use dialogue
- Use drama
- Read aloud

*Kinaesthetic learners:*
- Be practical
- Use three-dimensional models
- Make things
- Use tactile experience
- Move about
- Write

*Visual learners:*
- Use pictures
- Use diagrams
- Use colour coding
- Use highlighting
- Use handouts
- Do practical demonstrations

## Subject areas

In considering different subject areas there are some common points and some points that are specific to certain areas. In all areas there is the need to teach unfamiliar subject-specific words. Because dyslexics need more rehearsal to remember new words and what they mean, it is important to build in re-capping and revising of specialist terms. In all areas children's written performance is unlikely to reflect their level of understanding and the critical issue is how the child gains access to the curriculum for that specialist area. It is important not to rule out more verbally based subjects as automatically unsuitable for dyslexic children to follow at formal examination level. W. B. Yeats, one of our greatest poets, had very poor literacy skills as a child and even as an adult had very weak spelling. A dyslexic student who graduated with a first class history degree said that although she was very slow learning to read, once she could read it was a source of great enjoyment, escapism and consolation to her and helped her survive her unhappy experiences at school. Motivation, interest and conceptual ability for a particular subject area should be kept to the forefront. Much of the emphasis at present is on the technical aspects of teaching, systematic monitoring, 'crisply' written IEPs, structured programmes of work, etc. This is essential as a foundation but the relationship that learners have with their teachers is equally important. Where a dyslexic student has a particular flair or interest in a subject area a positive relationship with the teacher of that subject can make a real difference to their experience of school and motivation to achieve.

*Last year his year tutor picked up on David's problem. He was really committed to helping David. He encouraged him with his marking and took a personal interest.*

## English

*Potential benefits:*
- Good visuo-spatial abilities when writing/reading information texts.
- Extremely high level of motivation and perseverance.
- Oral answers, group work participation.
- Good comprehension and understanding.
- Holistic thinking, and the ability to grasp the broad picture well, but without the detail.
- Unusual and creative strategies for approaching and managing learning.
- Ability to find unusual and creative solutions in problem-solving activities.

*Potential difficulties:*
- Significant discrepancy between verbal and written performance.
- Persistent or severe problems with spelling, and erratic spelling, even with 'easy' or common words.
- Difficulty in putting ideas down on paper.
- Problems ordering things sequentially.
- Trouble in following sequences or keeping track of place and line when reading.
- Difficulty in memorising facts, new terms, new names.
- Misreading or miscopying when taking notes.
- Mispronunciations and saying the wrong word even when the right word is known.
- Inability to read or extreme anxiety about reading aloud without preparation.
- Visuo-perceptual disturbances (words dance/float/blur/swirl when reading), scotopic sensitivity.
- Problems with sentence structure, punctuation and organisation of written work, not due to lack of experience.
- Need to re-read text numerous times to grasp and hold meaning.
- Inability to 'see' mistakes even when pointed out, but can usually identify them if text is read aloud.
- Increased difficulty in many of these areas when under stress (e.g. in exams); good days/bad days.

*Suggested strategies:*
- Praise and develop child's strengths.
- Listen to books on tape.
- Teach and use mindmaps to plan essays.
- Use dramatic improvisation.
- Hot-seat characters studied.
- Worksheets prepared with space size 12–14 Comic Sans font.
- Have a cue to let the pupil know what they will be asked to read in advance, having checked that the pupil will be able to succeed.
- Teach spelling rules.
- Revisit, recap and repeat teaching points using different teaching styles.
- Do not insist on reading aloud, make it an option.
- Teach subject-specific words.
- Vary activities and break up sustained activities into small tasks.
- Model how to write a particular piece of work.

- Explicitly teach reading techniques such as skimming and scanning.
- Use writing frames.
- Have dictionaries and thesaurus in class (teach children how to use and model).
- Cloze procedure.
- Text restructuring (showing the information in some other way).
- Text sequencing.
- Text prediction.
- Tape details of texts using own voice and use this for revision.
- Teach and provide ACE spelling dictionary.

## *Maths*

*Potential benefits:*
- Good visuo-spatial abilities, graphs and geometry.
- High level of motivation and perseverance.
- An unusually good grasp of mathematical logic.

*Potential difficulties:*
- Left–right confusions.
- Mathematical sign confusions.
- Making errors with numbers, for example writing them back to front (e.g. 34 as 43).
- Can have great difficulty remembering or writing sequences of numbers such as telephone numbers.
- Reading generally in maths, particularly in problems.
- Reading, spelling and writing maths words.
- Remembering times tables.
- Remembering basic number bonds.
- Understanding place value.
- Recognising the decimal point.
- Understanding fractions.
- An inability to transfer skills from one area to another.
- Telling the time.

Many of the difficulties dyslexic children encounter with mathematics are related to their poor short-term memory. This makes mental arithmetic and the learning of number facts and multiplication tables particularly difficult areas. As with literacy skills they often have much stronger conceptual abilities and understand the principles and logic of mathematics. Using a calculator (as long as there aren't input difficulties) helps them circumvent their mental arithmetic difficulties and enjoy the aspects of mathematics they are strong in.

*It really hurts (doing mental arithmetic), I try to hold the first number in my head but while I'm working out the next bit or trying to carry something on I've forgotten the first bit. Even if I close my eyes and use like all my energy it just doesn't come out ... I see stars and get really stressed ... algebra and geometry I'm OK at, I get really good marks.* (Lucy, very able 14-year-old)

*Suggested strategies (see also Chapter 3):*
- Whole-school approach provides better practical real-life mathematics.
- Teach subject-specific words.
- Use squared paper.
- Encourage the pupil to see the problem in their 'mind's eye'.
- Encourage the use of rulers to keep work tidy.
- Display clues for the topic being covered, words with explanations, examples of work.
- Make it fun, success breeds success.
- Teach for understanding.
- Emphasise estimation strategies to reduce short-term memory overload.
- Allow extended use of calculator.

# History

*Potential benefits:*
- Interest and enthusiasm.
- Good understanding of overview concepts.

*Potential difficulties:*
- Problems ordering things sequentially, particularly dates.
- Subject-specific words.
- Reading sources.

*Suggested strategies:*
- Dramatic improvisation.
- Projects.
- Teach subject-specific words.
- Use of tapes and video to complement sources.

# Music

*Potential benefits:*
- May excel.
- Raises self-esteem.
- Can relax.

*Potential difficulties:*
- Directional difficulties in following music.
- Weak phonological awareness.
- Difficulty learning to read music.

*Suggested strategies:*
- Singing may develop phonological awareness.
- Break words down to phonemes to match music.
- Give time to practise and develop confidence.
- Music may aid memory.
- Mnemonics to learn key words or sequences.
- Avoid the obvious left-hand/right-hand laterality problem.
- Don't overload the pupil with too many directions.
- Singing and choral experiences can be supportive, as they involve the separation of syllables – one of the main areas of difficulty in reading itself.
- Use of examination allowances.

## Geography

*Potential benefits:*
- Visual memory.
- Diagrams.
- Maps.
- Geography lends itself to short concise answers.

*Potential difficulties:*
- Visuo-perceptual disturbances when map reading.
- Weak working memory.

*Suggested strategies:*
- Teach subject-specific words.
- Videos.
- Colour and visual presentations.
- Diagrammatic form of written word.
- Pair up with a pupil to help/support.
- Discussion work.
- Textbooks that are visual.
- Read pupil's work for content.
- Word process course work.
- Encourage parental support.

## Science

*Potential benefits:*
- May be excellent at problem-solving.
- May enjoy practicals.
- May be well motivated.

*Potential difficulties:*
- Subject-specific vocabulary.
- Writing in the necessary style.
- Sequencing of ideas.

- Laying out practical write-ups correctly.

*Suggested strategies:*
- Teach subject-specific words.
- Display terms used in the unit of work.
- Provide writing frames.
- Practical work may aid memory.
- Use of colours.
- When reading ask the six questions: Who? What? Where? When? Why and How?
- Highlighter pens for key points or words.

## MFL (Modern Foreign Language)

*Potential benefits:*
- Raises self-esteem, the same as for everyone else.
- Some languages such as Italian and Spanish which are more 'phonologically transparent' should be easier to learn.

*Potential difficulties:*
- Spelling.
- Weak phonological skills.
- Working memory.
- Auditory discrimination.
- Syntax.
- Auditory sequencing.
- Speed of processing information.
- Attention span.
- Automaticity.

*Suggested strategies:*
- Use ICT.
- Teach keyboard skills (type to learn).
- Teach speaking and listening skills.

## Design Technology

*Potential benefits:*
- May be gifted in design and problem-solving.
- May be highly motivated.

*Potential difficulties:*
- Organisational.
- Sequential.
- Presentation of ideas.

*Suggested strategies:*
- Teach subject-specific words.

- Writing frames.
- Texts on tape.
- Use of ICT.

**ICT** *Potential benefits:*
- Child proud of work.
- Increased self-esteem.
- Spelling errors automatically signalled by computer in red.
- Green line to identify grammatical errors.
- Good keyboard skills allow child to realise potential.
- Good keyboard skills give work much better level of presentation.
- Good keyboard skills allow child to work faster.
- Good keyboard skills are less tiring than handwriting.
- Allows better organisation of work through cutting, pasting and revision.

*Potential difficulties:*
- Child does not know which spellchecker suggestion to select.
- Weak spelling hinders use of www.
- Poor keyboard skills slow down child and lead to clerical errors.

*Suggested strategies:*
- Teach subject-specific words.
- Teach keyboard skills, do not expect child to just pick them up.
- Talkback software.
- Speech to text software.
- Be willing to try a range of software as there is no one best way; the individual needs to dictate the best software.

This information is in no way definitive. Each child is different; the challenge is for subject areas to work collectively on support to enable access to their area. The list of potential difficulties can sometimes appear daunting to subject area teachers. The important point is that many dyslexic children will have much better conceptual skills than reading and writing skills. Perhaps because dyslexia is a 'hidden' disability it is harder to appreciate that most of the difficulties are in terms of access to the curriculum not in learning the subject area. The specific learning difficulty is largely in the mechanics of reading and writing; the challenge for the subject teacher is how to circumvent or provide support for this. Teaching which emphasises thinking skills, understanding, and logical analysis will allow dyslexic children to use their stronger conceptual abilities and demonstrate their learning ability. Teaching based heavily on rote learning and the copying of facts and figures will put their poorer short-term memory and lack of automaticity under stress and will not enable them to use their better conceptual ability in order to learn. Dyslexic university students (Riddick *et al.* 1997) were asked to rate on a five-point scale how well they did in their GCSEs and A levels compared to the predictions made for them by their teachers. In comparison to matched non-dyslexic students they rated themselves as doing better than their teachers expected whereas non-dyslexic students as a group said they did slightly worse than their teachers expected. This underlines the importance of not underestimating dyslexic children and not being unduly influenced by the 'poor' appearance of handwritten classwork. Many teachers are astonished at the difference in quality between handwritten and word-processed work of some dyslexic children.

> *I must admit the first time, I thought his mother must have written it. But he's done several pieces now, some started in school and finished at home … I can see it's his own work. It's completely changed my view of what he's capable of, really I underestimated him, totally underestimated him.*

Word-processing plays a critical role for many dyslexic children in giving them greater pride in their own work and changing the teachers' perceptions of what they are capable of.

## Whole-school approaches

It is through whole-school approaches that most success can be achieved and difficulties overcome. If a child is taught how to do graphs in maths and then again in geography, history and PSHE, over-learning can be achieved. However, it must be stressed, the same methods must be taught. 'Do it this way in my subject area' or 'forget what you learnt in geography, this is how we do it in maths' can only confuse and further 'pigeonhole' learning. Real learning goes beyond subject boundaries and pulls together what has been learnt so that it can be applied in differing situations.

## Metacognition

Metacognitive approaches stress the importance of the student's self-knowledge of what is to be learnt and how they learn. Effective learners are those who are quite clear about what the task demands and know how well they can meet it.

Since Flavell (1977) coined the term 'metacognition', an individual's conscious awareness of their own thought processes, there has been a great deal of research on thinking about thinking. It has been demonstrated that young children and low achievers are less able than adults to talk about techniques and methods of learning and problem-solving. If learners can become more aware of their own thought processes and learning strategies, they should gain conscious control over them, as well as the ability to widen their range of strategies. This could provide the key to transfer and generalisation, as both are somewhat restricted in a compartmentalised curriculum. Campione *et al.* (1995) have summarised suggestions on how to teach transferable skills, so that they do, in fact, transfer. They include the need to:

- use discovery learning methods to promote pupil involvement and meaningful learning;
- raise awareness of the possibilities for transfer and provide explicit examples;
- use many and varied examples and training contexts.

Feuerstein's (1988) main vehicle for transfer uses bridging. He suggests that at the end of a lesson students might be provoked into thinking about how they would tackle analogous problems well beyond the original learning context. This way they increase the use of metacognition.

Self-regulation is an important aspect of metacognition as it allows decisions to be made about the existence of a problem, the demands of the task and the need for a strategy to be found as a solution.

Literacy taught across curriculum areas can have benefits, as a child can develop reading and spelling in an area associated with success and pleasure rather than receiving more of the same work from the English teacher. The provision of dictionaries and thesauruses in all subject areas can only benefit all children.

Study skills are of benefit to all children but are essential for many children with dyslexia.

## IEPs

The IEP contains information which teachers can use to inform effective planning and ensure access to the curriculum. It is written after involving parents and pupils so all involved know what is expected.

The IEP should clearly fit that individual and the use of proformas for different learning difficulties will not be individual. We like the idea that IEP also stands for 'implementing effective practice'. The rationale for IEPs is simple; they provide a means whereby additional SEN provision can be detailed and its effectiveness systematically monitored. The IEP should clearly state the nature of the student's difficulty, the student's learning styles, suggested strategies and targets which will be used as measures of success when the IEP is reviewed.

Assessment for IEP planning should be part of whole-school planning and should aim to ensure that IEP targets are set within the context of the statutory target setting for overall pupil performance which came into effect in September 1998. Dyslexic students' difficulties change over time, mainly due to curriculum demands, which are linked to Key Stage level of study priorities.

Typically dyslexic students need targets and additional provision which are based on their 'past, present and future' needs. They need to regularly revisit areas of work from the previous term or Key Stage; they need to work on specific areas from their current learning objectives; and they need to prepare for the curricular and organisational demands of the next Key Stage.

Progress in reading and writing for dyslexic students is noticeably slower than for non-dyslexic students and this needs to be acknowledged when writing targets.

As Tod (1999) says, IEPs bring precision and rigour to the planning and monitoring of 'additional or otherwise extra' provision. Such provision should impact upon pupil progress and enable pupils with dyslexia to develop the skills and strategies needed for lifelong learning. However, there is a need to refine and increase staff access to and involvement in the production of IEPs, implementing classroom practice as a result of the IEP and evaluation of their own practice as well as the provision for the student.

The IEPs which follow are not being presented as perfect working examples but as genuine working documents from a mainstream comprehensive. To maintain confidentiality, children's names have been changed.

# Individual Education Plan

**Name** Mark Boy
**Area/s of concern** Learning weak auditory memory/Behaviour

**Start date** Jan 2002
**Proposed support**

**Stage** School Action
**Year** 7
**Review Date** 13/02/02
**Support began** Year 7

| Targets | Achievement Criteria | Possible resources and techniques | Possible strategies for use in class | Ideas for support teacher /assistant | Outcome |
|---|---|---|---|---|---|
| 1 To use visualisation to aid memory of lists of words. | 1 To remember 5 words from a list. | 1 Pictures. Word lists. List memory games e.g. 'I went shopping . . .'. | 1 Talk about strategies for memorising. Give examples of how to use visualisation. | 1 Explain how to use visualisation. Play games to reinforce. | |
| 2 Mark to understand and conform to school rules and sanctions. | 2 Improvement in compliance by the end of next half term. | 2 Establish clear rules for classroom and display. | 2 Discuss rules with class and pupil. Refer to rules when managing pupil. | 2 Praise and rewards for following rules. | |
| 3 To follow instructions given by adults on duty at break times. | 3 Good response noted by teachers on duty over a period of half a term. | 3 Record book. Reward system. Positive feedback. | 3 Look at record book with Mark. Comment positively on any good reports. | 3 Talk about different scenarios with Mark. Discuss ways of responding. | |
| 4 To make use of diary to organise: homework/ exams/study schedule /events. | 4 Noted to use diary daily. | 4 Diary. Picture prompts. | 4 Talk about how to use a diary. Encourage Mark to refer to it when necessary. | 4 Discuss the use of a diary. Ensure tasks are written in, ticked off when completed. | |

**Parents/carers need to** Help Mark to learn any words sent home. Parents to reinforce progress and support school in applying any sanctions needed. Look at diary to check it has been used, homework recorded and completed, and deadlines met.

**Student needs to** Use visualisation when remembering. Listen to instructions. Show the diary at home. Write things in diary and complete homework. Pack school bag for the following day.

# Individual Education Plan

| | |
|---|---|
| **Name** | Luke White |
| **Area/s of concern** | Dyslexia which affects Luke's access to the curriculum due to poor literacy skills, short-term memory and low self-esteem |
| **Supported by** | TA Maths, Science, English |

| | | | |
|---|---|---|---|
| **Start date** | Jan 2002 | **Stage** | Statement |
| **Proposed support** | Access to the curriculum and learning support. Praise and encouragement for class participation and work completed. | **Year** | 8 |
| | | **Review Date** | 14/12/01 |
| | | **Support began** | Primary school |

| | Targets | Achievement Criteria | Possible resources and techniques | Possible strategies for use in class | Ideas for support teacher/assistant | Outcome |
|---|---|---|---|---|---|---|
| 1 | To make 6 months' progress as measured on a standardised reading test. | Improved results shown on NFER reading test after an interval of 3 terms. | Reading books and activity sheets. High interest/low reading level books. Tape-recorded books. Computer software. Paired reading. | Give Luke opportunities to practise reading skills. Monitor progress. | Use multi-sensory methods to teach word attack skills. Encourage Luke to use all cues when reading. | |
| 2 | To use 'Look, say, cover, write, check' strategy to practise spellings. | Observed on 7 occasions. | Spelling books. Corrected written work. | Encourage Luke to use the strategy to learn words that have been corrected in his written work. | Make sure that Luke is using the strategy correctly. | |
| 3 | To know the following multiplication tables(s): 6 and 7. | Accurate when tested on three separate occasions. | 100 square to colour tables patterns. Tables tapes. Finger method. Cards with sum on one side, answer on the back. | Provide activities to reinforce knowledge. Set questions for instant recall response. Plot graphs of times tables. | Give practice in reciting tables. Build on those tables Luke already knows. Teach strategies to help him learn tables/refer to tables quickly. | |
| 4 | Accurate when tested on three separate occasions. | Long word jigsaws. Words with spaces between syllables. Compound words to split into component parts. | Give practice in reading and spelling the multi-syllable words, and looking at words within words. | Show Luke where to split multi-syllabic words. Give practice in pronouncing multi-syllabic words accurately. | | |

**Parents/carers need to** Listen to Luke read and ask questions about the text. Encourage Luke to proof read written work. Chant tables together.

**Student needs to** Read each day at school and at home. Practise any spellings sent home. Use tapes to learn tables.

# Individual Education Plan

**Name** Colin Cole
**Area/s of concern** Learning, weak verbal and visual memory

| | | **Stage** | School Action |
|---|---|---|---|
| | | **Year** | 9 |
| | | **Review Date** | 18/06/02 |
| **Supported by** | | **Support began** | January 2002 |
| **Start date** | Jan 2002 | | |

**Proposed support** Allow extra time for writing, using lined paper with margins. Maths use graph paper to assist setting out work. Sit near the whiteboard. Do not give too many verbal/visual instructions at one time – if necessary provide simple written instructions to have on the desk. Check understanding of instructions.

| Targets | Achievement Criteria | Possible resources and techniques | Possible strategies for use in class | Ideas for support-teacher /assistant | Outcome |
|---|---|---|---|---|---|
| 1 To use mind-mapping techniques to help with organisation of ideas. | 1 Organises information brainstormed on 8 occasions. | 1 Worksheets. Discussion. Brainstorming. | 1 Show mind-mapping techniques. Set group brainstorming lessons. | 1 Practise selecting and organising important information. | |
| 2 To use self-repetition to aid memory of words/ instructions. | 2 Repeats and remembers words/ instructions with 3 parts. | 2 Tape-recorder. Word lists. | 2 Talk about strategies for memorising. Give examples of how to use repetition. | 2 Explain how to use repetition. Play games to reinforce. | |

**Parents/carers need to** Encourage mind-mapping to organise thoughts, praise and encouragement. Encourage repetition.

**Student needs to** Use mind-mapping when doing homework. Practise repeating things he wants to remember onto a tape.

# Individual Education Plan

| | |
|---|---|
| **Name** | Michael Quill |
| **Area/s of concern** | Dyslexia, behaviour |
| **Supported by** | |

| | |
|---|---|
| **Stage** | School Action |
| **Year** | 9 |
| **Review Date** | June 2002 |
| **Support began** | 01/01/02 |

| | **Start date** | Jan 2002 |
|---|---|---|
| | **Proposed support** | Michael has very weak visual memory but a slightly better auditory memory. He is a kinaesthetic learner. Please give extra time to complete tasks. Encourage planning, organisation, word processing work. Give praise and encouragement. |

| Targets | Achievement Criteria | Possible resources and techniques | Possible strategies for use in class | Ideas for support teacher /assistant | Outcome |
|---|---|---|---|---|---|
| 1 To use mind-mapping techniques to help with organisation of ideas. | 1 Organises information brainstormed on 8 occasions. | 1 Worksheets. Discussion. Brainstorming. | 1 Show mind-mapping techniques. Set group brainstorming lessons. | 1 Practise selecting and organising important information. | |
| 2 To learn and use strategies for taking notes from texts. | 2 Three pieces of work completed. | 2 Suitable texts for practice. Information sheets showing methods of note-taking. | 2 Set exercises for note taking. Talk about ways of taking notes. Praise efforts to apply strategies learnt. | 2 Teach strategies that suit Michael's way of learning. Photocopy texts for highlighting important points. | |
| 3 To make use of diary to organise: homework/ exams/study schedule/ events. | 3 Noted to use diary daily by it being checked on Wednesdays by Mr Hardie. | 3 Diary. | 3 Talk about how to use a diary. Encourage Michael to refer to it when necessary. | 3 Discuss the use of a diary. Ensure tasks are written in, ticked off when completed. | |

**Parents/carers need to** Encourage mind-mapping techniques, praise and encouragement. Look at diary to check use and work done. Encourage use of Type to Learn at home to develop keyboard skills.

**Student needs to** Use mind-mapping when doing homework. Try to apply strategies learnt. Show the diary at home. Write things in diary. Use Type to Learn to develop keyboard skills.

# Individual Education Plan

| Name | Mark Hall | Stage | Statement |
|---|---|---|---|
| Area/s of concern | Dyslexia/Emotional/Behavioural | Year | 8 |
| Supported by | SENCO each morning before school | Review Date | 14/12/01 |
| | LSAs 5 hours a week in class support | Support began | Sept 01 |
| | Start date | Oct 2001 | |
| | Proposed support | Disapplied from French. Sound linkage and SRA corrective reading. Units of Sound and Star spell program. | |

| Targets | Achievement Criteria | Possible resources and techniques | Possible strategies for use in class | Ideas for support teacher /assistant | Outcome |
|---|---|---|---|---|---|
| 1 To make 6 months' progress as measured on a standardised reading test. | 1 Improved results shown on NFER reading test after an interval of three terms. | 1 Reading books and activity sheets. High interest/ low reading level books. Tape-recorded books. Computer software. Paired reading. | 1 Give Mark opportunities to practise reading skills. Monitor progress. | 1 Use multi-sensory methods to teach word attack skills. Encourage Mark to use all cues when reading. | |
| 2 To listen to the teacher and get on with his work without delaying tactics. | 2 Work is begun within 2 minutes on 8 separate occasions. | 2 Monitoring chart. Clear expectations. | 2 Give brief, clear explanations at the start. Encourage starting work straight away. Positive comments. | 2 Check that Mark understands what he is required to do. Go through monitoring chart with him. Praise achievement. | |
| 3 To identify the beginning and end sound of a spoken word. | 3 Accurate when tested at random on three separate consecutive occasions. | 3 I-Spy. Dictated words. Point and match. Games. Wooden/plastic letters. Sound linkage. | 3 Check that initial and final sounds are heard correctly. Encourage the use of phonic attack when reading. | 3 Provide opportunity for Mark to show that the sounds have been recognised. | |
| 4 To control his temper when he is annoyed. | 4 Fewer than 5 incidents of loss of temper observed over a period of 7 weeks. | 4 Role-play. Discussion. Time out. | 4 Discuss temper control. Arrange for a safe place for Mark to go to calm down. | 4 Discuss feelings with Mark. Teach tactics for controlling temper. | |

**Parents/carers need to** Listen to Mark read and ask questions about the text. Encourage cooperation. Play I-Spy using the initial sounds. Discuss temper control.

**Student needs to** Settle to task quickly. Be aware of the targets.

Note taking can have particular problems for the child who has a weak working memory. Thought should be given to mind map teaching, use of Dictaphone or tape recording. Handing the child a copy of the teacher's notes before the lesson gives the opportunity for the child to read through in preparation for the lesson. During the lesson the teacher can build on the content of the notes, helping access to the lesson, as well as revisit the content to develop automaticity and improve self-confidence.

*General literacy issues such as note taking*

Copying from the board or OHP may have particular difficulties for a child with scotopic sensitivity, sequence difficulties and weak working memory. Give handouts if possible before the lesson so the child arrives with prior knowledge of what is to be learnt. This also enables an overview of the lesson before chunking down and gives a reason and purpose for the lesson.

*Copying from the board*

Use two pens, neither red, one for ideas/content, the other for 'surface' structure. Be sensitive, many students with SpLD have been badly hurt by lack of understanding in the past.

Explain what is required and what went wrong; use clear, explicit English avoiding innuendo, sarcasm and complex sentence structure; avoid using grammatical terms.

A pupil with dyslexia is unlikely to know how to correct or improve an error without some guidance, model or explanation; they are not usually familiar with grammatical terms or rules.

*Teacher's policy on marking*

These comments are taken from class books:

> *Concentrate on the detail of the answer, Sally. I can see you understand the work but an examiner would not be so generous. Well done though.*

> *Well done John, excellent effort.*

> *Improving work. Well done Billy.*

*Examples of constructive marking comments*

The school environment is a complex place where there are many different parts, each affecting the other. However, the strategies which enable a dyslexic student will also enable other

*Specific interventions*

students to learn and have success at school. No one single approach holds the key, it may be a combination of programmes and strategies working with other teaching and curriculum approaches that brings success for the dyslexic student.

The importance of access to the curriculum in whole-class teaching, which is where students spend most of their time when at school, cannot be overemphasised. A successful withdrawn 30 minutes or an hour must also have links with the rest of the curriculum encourage independent learning and be cross-curricular.

## *Multi-sensory teaching*

Multi-sensory methods seek to stimulate all available senses simultaneously. One of the most well-known examples of a multi-sensory method is the 'look, say (trace finger over), cover, write, check' approach, which is often used to teach spellings.

Multi-sensory approaches for dyslexics have been positively evaluated (Hornsby and Miles 1980, Hornsby and Farmer 1990). However, the effect of individual teaching, specialist teacher training, and parental support associated with the delivery of these methods also needs to be considered, as they are variables which could have contributed to the observed increase in student progress.

If traditional simultaneous multi-sensory teaching is used exclusively the student may concentrate on their strong sense at the expense of improving the relatively weak area.

## *Provision*

Pupils will be taught and if necessary supported in ability appropriate sets. In planning programmes for the pupil with dyslexia it is important to consider what approaches are appropriate to suit that particular pupil's strengths and weaknesses. These may include:

- An individual education plan setting realistic targets for the child's progress based on assessments.
- Informing the staff of the pupil's learning difficulties and offering advice and strategies for appropriate approaches.
- Precision teaching techniques; using the pupil's strengths to devise an individual programme based on his or her individual learning style.
- A structured reading programme with emphasis on phonics, such as Toe by Toe, Units of Sound and Wellington Square.
- A structured spelling programme using simultaneous oral

spelling, computer games to increase repetition, a personal dictionary and work on learning to use the ACE dictionary.

- The use of alternative methods of recording work with a Dictaphone, mind maps and access to ICT. Teaching keyboard skills through programs such as Type to Learn.
- Modified curriculum and disapplication when appropriate.

## *Examinations*

Dyslexic students may be entitled to an additional 25 per cent of time in exams. The justification for this is that since the fundamental nature of dyslexia is a slower than average rate of processing information then, clearly, dyslexic students are disadvantaged in timed conditions unless additional time is allowed. Many pupils say that the additional time is like 'gold dust'. Some students may require the use of word-processing facilities in addition to extra time. This would be granted, for example, to a dyslexic student who uses a PC for most of his/her written work and whose ability to produce legible and coherent scripts under timed conditions would be particularly hampered without the use of a PC.

## *Class tests*

'Exams' also includes any form of 'class test', no matter how short it may be. It is imperative that teachers organising such tests allow for dyslexic students to have the additional time to which they are entitled, and check with pupils beforehand to ensure that provision is being met. This is equally applicable to any pupil in the class who may have other disabilities, hidden or otherwise.

## *Memory*

Memory has been cited as being more important than IQ in predicting GCSE results and limited research has been undertaken into promoting classroom teaching approaches which foster and enhance memory capacity and efficiency. Dyslexic students experience specific difficulty with remembering, retaining and recalling information. The most common problem with working memory is 'overload' caused by the fact that the dyslexic student has not automated the basic decoding skills needed for literacy.

Active processing enhances memory skills, and activities such as the use of mnemonics (auditory and/or visual) and mind mapping (Buzan 1993) support this.

## Accommodations for exams. When should reports be prepared?

Accommodations can be applied for during SATs and a history of these will help inform further provision. Any extra time the pupil is allowed needs to be built into school exams as well as public exams so that the pupil can practise using the time and it can become a normal part of their exam experience. Thought must also be given to the room these allowances are to be used in. Extra time in a large school hall may give equal opportunity but in no way is this equitable. A separated room is recommended which has been previously used for mock or other examinations prior to the external examination.

If a psychological assessment report is more than two years old it can be updated with a 'Supplementary Report' which tells the Board just about the important things and whether the candidate's levels of literacy and numeracy have changed.

The ideal time to apply for examination allowances is at the end of Year 9 before beginning GCSE coursework so that any allowance can be incorporated into the course. This prevents over-testing of candidates as they can be reassessed before embarking on GCE A levels.

The Board will want a report signed by a psychologist, or by a teacher who has taken one of a list of specialist training courses (the BDA has the list of courses if you want to check).

## The report should have information on:

- *Reading speed*: Do candidates read so slowly that they lose the sense of the question?
- Do they read so slowly that they spend considerably more time reading the questions than their peers do? This is particularly important if the exam has special passages to be read before answering the questions.
- *Reading accuracy*: If candidates feel that they are under pressure do they read inaccurately? If they know they have extra time, does it help?
- *Spelling*: Does an attempt at accurate spelling slow candidates' writing? Are there words they spell 'strangely' but consistently? Do they use words that are easy to spell rather than the 'best' word? Is spelling so difficult for them that they need someone to 'translate' it?
- *Handwriting speed:* Is the speed at which candidates write so slow that they need more time? If so, has someone tried to teach them how to use as few words as possible to say what they mean? If they take a long time to write, ask for a time allowance.
- *Handwriting legibility:* Again, is the writing readable if the candidates don't feel under pressure? Extra time would

then be appropriate. If not, is it so illegible that it needs 'translating'? Amanuensis or the use of a word processor may be the answer in such cases.

- *Other difficulties*: We know that dyslexia has many effects on the learning process as well as causing difficulty with reading, writing and sometimes areas of numeracy. Problems with understanding language spoken at speed, short-term memory and sequencing for example can make life difficult for dyslexic candidates.

If you and the school have found that such candidates need additional support with specific areas due to these weaknesses, then you can ask the Board to let them have that help in the coursework and/or exams. You will need a psychologist or specialist to say how the candidates will be affected; what help has been tried and how it has helped and how this fits in with any test requirements.

## Dyslexia and careers

The Connexions Service now has a particular brief to help and support students who have experienced difficulties at school. They should be involved before options are chosen in Key Stage 4 and as necessary throughout the child's final years at school. Their input can be very helpful in motivating the young person to achieve in school so that they can attend further or higher education, where higher thinking skills are necessary rather than the basic skills frequently revisited in the school setting.

## Acknowledgement

I wish to acknowledge the contribution made to this chapter and to the success of pupils by all the staff of Saint Wilfrid's RC Comprehensive School.

*Chapter 5*

# Raising Self-esteem

Children with a range of special needs are at greater risk of developing low self-esteem (Elbaum and Vaughn 2001). However, there are two factors related to dyslexia which make dyslexic children particularly vulnerable to low self-esteem:

- Literacy performance is central to educational performance.
- Some have additional difficulties with coordination or organisation.

Early studies which compared the self-esteem of dyslexic and non-dyslexic children found that the dyslexic children had lower self-esteem on average (Rosenthal 1973, Thomson and Hartley 1980). Despite increasing awareness of dyslexia, recent studies in Britain, Europe and the USA have still found lower self-esteem in dyslexic children, students and adults (Gjessing and Karlsen 1989, Casey *et al.* 1992, Lewandowski and Arcangelo 1994, Riddick *et al.* 1999, Humphrey 2002). These studies look at differences at the group level and it is clear that there are big individual differences between people with dyslexia when it comes to self-esteem. These differences seem to be related to a number of risk and protective factors, with positive experiences at primary and secondary school counting as an important protective factor:

| *Protective factors* | *Risk factors* |
|---|---|
| Parental support | Lack of parental support |
| Early identification | Late identification |
| Early educational support | Lack of early educational support |

| | |
|---|---|
| Positive experience at primary school | Negative experience at primary school |
| Positive experience at secondary school | Negative experience at secondary school |
| High self-esteem | Low self-esteem |
| Special talent or skill | No special skill or talent identified |
| Supportive friends | Socially isolated |
| Friends or role models with similar difficulties | No similar friends or role models |
| Teacher or other adult who believes in the child and acts as a benefactor | No special adult benefactor |
| Good coping strategies | Poor coping strategies |

## The role of self-esteem

Self-esteem is important because it influences general well-being, goal setting, motivation and social interaction. Persistent low self-esteem is linked to low self-efficacy, anxiety and depression. Coopersmith (1967) was one of the first to research self-esteem in children. He found that young children with high self-esteem expected to succeed at tasks, would ask for adult help and had more confidence in their own responses. Children low in self-esteem were hesitant and apprehensive when faced with new tasks they did not expect to succeed at and were more likely to give up easily or be unduly influenced by their peers.

A mother who considered her dyslexic son to have very low self-esteem partly because he had constantly been called lazy at primary school made the following comment:

> *What I find difficult to get through to certain teachers is that he's had so many negatives that the positives aren't enough. The problem is they need to improve his self-esteem or he won't even try. If he thinks he's going to fail then he won't try in the beginning.* (Riddick 1996: 105)

For some children it is easy to see how they get into a vicious circle where they give up trying with literacy skills because they have had so little success, the resultant lack of practice (see Chapter 1) only exacerbating the gap between their performance and the performance of their peers.

Lawrence (1987) carried out a series of studies on children with reading disabilities. He concluded that: 'The relationship between reading attainment and self-esteem is a reciprocal one with each affecting the other' (Lawrence 1987: 64).

The basic issue for teachers, parents and children is where to break into this circle and start to change a child's behaviour and experiences. For all children it is essential that they get help with their specific learning difficulties but for some, additional attention needs to be paid to their low self-esteem and consequent approach to learning. As well as comparing themselves unfavourably with other children in terms of literacy skills many dyslexic children also have coordination difficulties. Children with dyspraxia or motor coordination problems often find it difficult to join in with playground games and sports and in consequence their social relations with other children and their self-esteem suffer (Ripley *et al.* 1997). A number of studies have shown that children with coordination problems are more likely to be bullied and teased, especially in the playground.

## *Attributions*

Attributions are the reasons or explanations someone gives for their own performance or the performance of someone else. A child, for example, could attribute doing well in an exam to luck (the right questions came up) or to hard work. The first is an external and uncontrollable attribution whereas the second is an internal and controllable attribution. Children who have a history of failure are more likely to attribute any success they have to luck and to attribute failure to permanent deficiencies in themselves. In other words they blame themselves for any failures. This can set up a feeling of learned helplessness where children think there is nothing they can do that can change the situation so they give up trying at all.

For some children it is important to help them change their attributional style to one that stresses that any successes are down to their own abilities and efforts. Targeted intensive teaching that demonstrates to a child that through extra effort they can succeed may be one way of starting to change a child's attribution style. IEPs can also play an important part in this process by selecting achievable targets for children, especially where children have been genuinely involved in deciding on their targets.

It is also important to give verbal or written feedback in a form that attributes success to internal controllable factors such as the effort or imagination that a child has put into a piece of work:

*Well done Kylie, you have worked hard to produce an excellent piece of writing.*

*Great work Sean, the extra work on capital letters has really paid off, you used them seven times out of nine, see if you can beat that score next time.*

Give targeted attainable literacy goals:

- In written feedback link praise to internal controllable attributes (e.g. effort, ability, etc.).
- Give the child alternative attributions which challenge negative thinking.

Interviews with mothers of dyslexic children revealed that a key thing that many of them did was to try and counter negative attributions that their children made.

## Educationalists' attributions

Attributions are a normal part of individuals' lives; they use them to try and make sense of why other individuals have behaved in a certain way: 'She did that because she was upset about her mother being ill' (external, changeable attribution).

Educationalists have to use attributions to help them explain, predict and respond to the behaviour of the children they are teaching. The reason why a child is behaving or performing in a certain way will have a strong influence on how a teacher responds to that child. One of the problems with dyslexia is that it is a 'hidden' or not 'evident' disability so a child's difficulty in learning to read or spell can mistakenly be attributed to lack of effort, experience or ability. It can be argued that one of the important points about the construct of dyslexia is that it challenges these negative and inaccurate attributions and suggests more accurate and constructive attributions which can be used to inform the approach to teaching. Many dyslexic children and adults feel the label 'dyslexia' stops them blaming themselves and in the right circumstances helps them to view themselves more positively:

*It was great it wasn't my fault any longer, I wasn't to blame.* (Dalgit, 11 years)

Dyslexic children, students and their parents report over and over again that they have been called or made to feel the following by teachers:

- stupid
- lazy
- careless
- slow

- messy
- idiotic

*There was a lesson with double history, all she did was write on the board and you had to answer questions and look at a textbook and I sat next to a girl, she wouldn't let anyone see her work and I used to just sit there and the teacher afterwards would just have a go at me saying how stupid I was and stuff like that.*

*The first year there they called me all those names but then I did an exam and I came out, I was like in the top ten out of the whole year and then they stopped calling me stupid, they just called me lazy.* (Laura, 15 years)

## Self-esteem

It has been suggested that self-esteem starts as a global concept with a very young child feeling they are basically worthy or unworthy. But as children get older they may start to differentiate between different aspects of their experience with the consequence that self-esteem may be relatively higher in some areas than others.

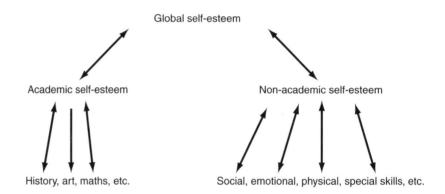

An important point is that self-esteem is related to those areas of endeavour that a person particularly values or aspires to be competent or significant in. In terms of personal interests, pastimes or hobbies, children have considerable freedom to pursue those activities that give them enjoyment and a sense of competence. A child with poor reading and writing skills can spend their time for instance playing imaginative games, putting together lego-technic models or developing a sporting skill such as swimming or skating. A child with poor motor coordination could focus on good social interaction skills, designing computer graphics, helping on a city farm, etc. The difficulty for children in school is that in the formal curriculum they cannot escape the requirements for competent literacy skills and in the informal curriculum poor motor skills can lead to teasing or social exclusion.

*I felt like I was not like one of them, and when you don't know anything and the other kids know more than you, you think you are the lowest thing on earth.* (Jamie, 8 years) (Riddick 2000)

Pre-school children tend to have fairly high self-esteem but over the first few years of schooling their self-esteem often drops as they begin to make social comparisons with other children (Marsh 1990). It's not hard to imagine that the difficulties that dyslexic children encounter in learning to read, spell and write will lead them to make a number of negative comparisons of themselves in relation to other more 'competent' children in their class. In interviewing dyslexic students Riddick *et al.* (1997) found that several recalled incidences from 12 to 30 years in the past where they had made a negative social comparison between themselves and other children because they were on a 'lower' reading book. Both children and students indicated that it was visible public indicators like being the last to finish reading a handout or finishing a piece of written work that particularly affected them. This sense of humiliation could be exacerbated if negative attention was drawn to their performance by an adult in authority.

*One of my lasting memories of junior school is that I produced a piece of work that looked fine to me ... and the teacher came back into the class and said 'Everyone's done a wonderful piece of work except for one person and that person is Andy and I want him to come out and hold up his book so the rest of the class can see it'. So I dragged myself up and again this feeling of being so small, so stupid.* (Andy, university student, 27 years of age) (Riddick *et al.* 1997: 35)

*I don't like being shown up in front of the class. The spelling tests are the worst. I'm not frightened of the shouting, but I don't like it when they get the class to laugh, like one teacher used to do.* (Michelle, Year 7, 11 years of age) (Riddick 1996: 135)

Although it would be hoped that experiences like these were becoming less common, in recent research Humphrey (2002) found that half of 63 dyslexic children spoken to reported that they had been criticised or humiliated by teachers. This often happened before children were identified as dyslexic with incorrect attributions being made that they were either 'lazy' or 'stupid'. Humphrey compared dyslexic children who were attending specialist units with dyslexic and non-dyslexic children in mainstream schools. Differences were found in self-esteem between dyslexic and non-dyslexic children but these were strongly moderated by situational factors. The dyslexic children in mainstream schools had significantly lower self-esteem than the dyslexic children in specialist units. Humphrey suggested that this was because the specialist units provided a much more dyslexia friendly environment and children were comparing themselves to other children with similar difficulties. This endorses the findings of Thomson (1990), who assessed the self-esteem of a group of dyslexic children prior to them attending a specialist dyslexia school, and groups of dyslexic children who had attended the specialist school for 6 months (1st group) and 18 months (2nd group). He found that the children who had attended the school for 18 months had the highest self-esteem and that prior to attending the specialist school children had very low self-esteem.

| Self-esteem | General | Social | Academic | Parental |
|---|---|---|---|---|
| 1st group | 50% | 32% | 45% | 87% |
| 2nd group | 60% | 84% | 77% | 87% |

In order to assess children's self-esteem Thomson used the Battle (1992) Culture-Free Self-esteem Inventory (CFSE) (see also p. 96). This has four sub-scales for general, social, academic and parental self-esteem. What is notable is that children had high parental self-esteem from the beginning, in other words they felt valued and supported by their parents. Their low social and academic esteem were closely tied to their experiences at mainstream schools. Whereas low academic self-esteem in dyslexic children may not seem too surprising, low social self-esteem may seem on the surface to be more surprising. But comments from dyslexic children and adults make it clear that in being compared unfavourably with other children they often feel worthless and humiliated. This in turn leads to children feeling isolated or different from other children; some lose all confidence and withdraw from other children, others feel angry and frustrated.

> *I knew I was different from the other children, I got more and more punished and humiliated, so I actually withdrew into myself and became so ashamed that by the age of eight I had withdrawn so much ... I was frightened of other people finding out I had an English problem and I really went into a world of my own. I didn't have any friends, I was too ashamed.* (June, mature university student describing her experience at school when she was 8 years old)

The encouraging point is that in the right environments dyslexic children can have relatively high self-esteem. The challenge is how to create such an environment in mainstream schools.

Ben, the student described in Chapter 1, had his self-esteem assessed at 7 years of age when he had a teacher who was very critical of his work and did not believe in dyslexia. At this time he was very demoralised and anxious in school and when observed by an educational psychologist was seen to spend a lot of time 'off target' and apparently 'daydreaming'. When re-tested at the age of 17 he had received several years of specific targeted literacy and study skills teaching within a mainstream school environment that was positive and supportive in its approach to children with dyslexia. He was now achieving at a standard commensurate with his academic ability, and felt a valued part of the school community. He commented spontaneously that his self-esteem was much higher than it had been in the past.

Ben's scores on the Battle Culture-Free Self-esteem Inventory Form A (see p. 96) are shown in the table below.

| Self-esteem | General | Social | Academic | Parental |
|---|---|---|---|---|
| Age 7 | Very Low | Low | Very Low | High |
| Age 17 | High | High | High | High |

## Assessing self-esteem

Although teacher observations can identify some children who obviously have low self-esteem they can overlook other children who simply do not draw attention to themselves or hide their distress and lack of confidence under a facade. Using a self-esteem inventory can be a useful adjunct to other forms of information. Most contemporary self-esteem inventories have separate sub-scales so that different aspects of a child's self-esteem can be considered. Self-esteem inventories can help inform and assess support for individual children or assess new school developments such as changes in the way learning support is delivered.

Understandably some children are defensive or wary when asked personal questions so inventories often contain some questions that deliberately set out to check for this. In the CFSE inventory for example there is a defensiveness (lie) scale made up of questions such as:

- I never do anything wrong
- I like everybody I know, etc.

If a child answers yes to a high proportion of these questions they are deemed to be defensive and the tester would be cautious in interpreting the child's overall scores. Well-standardised inventories like the Marsh (1990) or the CFSE (Battle 1992) make it possible to compare both overall self-esteem and its various sub-scales against norms for children in general. Although it is useful to consider various areas of self-esteem, many would argue that most children have an underlying global perception of themselves as either worthy or unworthy. Harter (1985) demonstrated that in some cases children could have very similar profiles for individual areas of self-esteem but still have very different self-worth scores.

Because of the literacy difficulties that dyslexic children have, these kinds of assessment often need some adaptation. For some children simply enlarging the form and/or placing a guide under each question in turn is sufficient.

## The Culture-Free Self-esteem Inventory (Battle 1992)

The CFSE comes in a short form (30 questions) and a long form (60 questions) for children. The questions are designed to tap four different areas of children's self-esteem and as already mentioned there is a lie scale to check for defensiveness. General self-esteem is taken to be the overall perception children have of their own worth. Social self-esteem focuses on how valued a child feels by their peers, and parental self-esteem similarly examines how valued a child feels by their parents. Academic self-esteem relates to how well a child thinks they are doing in formal areas of learning.

|  | Short Form B | Long Form A | Sample question |
|---|---|---|---|
| General | 10 questions | 20 questions | I worry a lot |
| Social | 5 questions | 10 questions | I only have a few friends |
| Academic | 5 questions | 10 questions | I often feel like leaving school |
| Parental | 5 questions | 10 questions | My parents think I am a failure |
| Lie | 5 questions | 10 questions | I never worry about anything |

Children are asked to tick either the YES or NO box at the end of each question. The short form, as the name implies, has fewer questions (30 in total) and is therefore less taxing for anyone with reading difficulties. Although there are British as well as US norms for this inventory, the questions still contain a few American words such as 'quit' and 'smarter'. These can be substituted with suitable English words such as 'give up' and 'cleverer'. There is also a taped version for use with younger children or children with reading difficulties. Children simply listen to each question in turn and tick the yes/no answer box, although some children will need a guide under each question so that their response is in the correct answer box. The taped version comes with an American accent so one school has made its own version using an English accent and slightly slower pace to give dyslexic children more time to respond. Battle has standardised the inventory on children from age 7 to 18 years who are still in the school environment. The adult version is standardised for use from 16 years upwards so discretion can be used in deciding which version would be most appropriate with older pupils. Whereas the children's version includes academic and parental sub-scales the adult version does not, which makes it less useful in an educational context. On the other hand some 16–18-year-olds might find a few of the questions on the children's version, particularly on the long form, a little young, or inappropriate for them, e.g. I have lots of fun with my parents.

There are also tables which allow both the overall score and the sub-test scores to be classified as:

Very High    High    Intermediate    Low    Very Low

## Self-Description Questionnaire (Marsh 1990)

This scale is standardised for use with children aged 8–12 years. There are 76 questions and these focus on three areas of academic self-concept and four areas of non-academic self-concept, as well as giving an overall score. This is rather lengthy and is perhaps better suited to research or monitoring purposes.

## The LAWSEQ Questionnaires (Lawrence 1987)

Lawrence (1987) has written specifically about enhancing self-esteem in the classroom. He has devised two quick and easy to administer questionnaires, one for primary age and one for secondary age children. These give a global score although the areas covered include social, academic, parental and general self-esteem:

*Primary version (sample questions)*

|  | Yes | No | Don't know |
|---|---|---|---|
| 1 Do you think that your parents usually like to hear about your ideas? | | | |
| 2 Do you often feel lonely at school? | | | |
| 3 Do other children often break friends or fall out with you? | | | |
| 4 Do you like team games? | | | |

Lawrence has standardised the questionnaires on both English and Australian children. He acknowledges the problems of reliability, especially where children give socially desirable answers, but claims that the brevity of these questionnaires does make them particularly useful for busy class teachers.

## Self-perception Profile for Children (Harter 1985)

Harter suggests that it is important to assess a child's overall feeling of self-worth as well as specific areas of self-esteem. Five areas of self-esteem are assessed with six questions on each area. In addition, six questions are asked about children's general sense of self-worth. This is called the Self-perception scale.

| | |
|---|---|
| *Social acceptance:* | How well regarded a child thinks they are by peers. |
| *Scholastic competence:* | How well a child thinks they are doing academically. |
| *Behavioural conduct:* | The extent to which a child thinks they adhere to their own standards of behaviour. |
| *Physical appearance:* | How far a child likes their own physical appearance. |
| *Athletic competence:* | How competent a child feels at physical and sporting activities. |

Harter was particularly concerned that children might want to give socially desirable answers and not admit to socially undesirable attributes. In order to try and overcome this issue she designed questions which described some children as being 'like this' and other children as being 'like that', and then asked a child to say which group of children he or she was most like.

| Really true for me | Sort of true for me | | | | Sort of true for me | Really true for me |
|---|---|---|---|---|---|---|
| 4 | 3 | Some kids are popular with others their age | BUT | Other kids are *not* very popular | 2 | 1 |
| 1 | 2 | Some kids have trouble figuring out the answers | BUT | Other kids almost *always* can figure out the answers | 3 | 4 |

At the end a graph-like profile of children's self-esteem in the five separate areas and overall self-worth can be produced. It is therefore easy to see in which areas children are feeling positive or negative about themselves.

In order to assess the self-esteem of younger children, Harter has produced a pictorial version for children under eight years. In this version the child is presented with two contrasting pictures of the same child, for example with or without many friends. Under each picture are two circles: the large one for 'a lot like me' and the small one for 'a little bit like me'.The child is asked to choose which child she is like and then to choose whether she is a lot like or a little bit like the child in the picture. This approach has obvious advantages for children with less advanced reading skills although some find the complexity of the layout and choice of response confusing.

## Informal methods

More informal methods ranging from talking to the child, getting groups of children together or playing games can be useful in obtaining a wider picture of how the child is feeling about things and especially any worries or difficulties they have in school. The 'All about me' game (Hemmings 1991) designed by Barnardos for children with possible family or school problems can be useful. This is a colourful board game which will appeal particularly to primary age children. The adult takes turns with the child in throwing a dice to move round the board. On each throw a card must be picked up and the question on it answered. A lot of the cards ask fun questions such as 'My favourite pop group is…'; 'What I'd most like for my birthday is…'. Some cards ask more serious questions such as: 'One thing that makes me sad is…'; I get frustrated when…'; 'Three things I'd like to tell my teacher are…'.

There are also some blank cards so specifically designed questions can be asked.

It is important to carry out the game in a collaborative manner with somebody the child feels relaxed with. It is also a good idea to start with several fun positive questions and spread more serious questions through the pile; this can be done by arranging the pile of cards in advance.

## Enhancing or maintaining self-esteem

At a simple level there are three aspects to this:

T – teach targeted literacy and organisational skills
E – environmental organisation to enhance access
A – attitudes and attributions

In talking to dyslexic children and adults it is apparent that what teachers should not do is as important to them as what they should do. When dyslexic children were asked to describe the best and the worst teachers they had encountered, their responses were very close to those given by most children, and many of the points they mentioned related to teachers' attitudes.

| *Best teacher* | *Worst teacher* |
| --- | --- |
| Encourages/praises | Cross/impatient/shouts |
| Helpful/adapts work/explains | Criticises or humiliates |
| Understanding/doesn't show you up | Not helpful/negative |
| Doesn't shout | Ignores/thinks you are useless |
| Sense of humour | Not understanding/insensitive |
| Knows child is dyslexic | Blames you, thinks you are lazy |

> *Well, teachers I like are helpful, the ones you can speak to and like they will treat you normal, they won't shout at you or anything if you do something wrong. Teachers who understand your problem and things like that. (Mason, 13 years)*

Many of the parents of dyslexic children identify at least one teacher who really 'believed' in their child and made a positive difference to how their child felt. Edwards (1994) found in the eight dyslexic boys she interviewed that they all emphasised the importance of a warm, trusting relationship with their teachers and several of them stressed the importance of having at least one teacher with whom they had an especially positive relationship.

Mason spoke of one teacher who had acted as his mentor and provided him with moral support.

*I got told off by my history teacher because I get on quite well with her, she said that if she was a person who was looking for someone to take (on a survival trip) and said she would probably take me because she said I'm good at talking, I'm very good at persuading people and good with my hands and things like that … she was just really saying like don't put yourself down, try your hardest and at the end of the day you will benefit.*

It is notable that in this snippet of conversation Mason's teacher is challenging his negative attributions and providing him with more positive ones.

## Do not

- Automatically attribute poor literacy and numeracy performance to lack of effort or ability.
- Verbally humiliate child in public.
- Organisationally humiliate (e.g. ask for spelling test scores in public).
- Ask child to read out loud in front of other children.
- Lay more emphasis on appearance than content of work.
- Assign child to an ability group on the basis of literacy rather than their thinking skills.
- Put red lines or corrections all over child's work.
- Ignore or undervalue child (e.g. work never prominently displayed because of untidy handwriting).
- Make insensitive jokes about the child's spelling or writing in public.

When dyslexic children were asked if there was anything they dreaded doing in school, reading out loud came first, closely followed by spelling tests. Two of the 16 dyslexic students that we interviewed claimed that they started truanting in secondary school in order to miss specific lessons in which they knew they would be required to read out loud (Riddick *et al.* 1997).

Sophie, a 15-year-old who was over five years behind in her reading accuracy, said that reading aloud was the thing that most concerned her at school:

*Reading out. In lessons they make you read out all the time. My mum does complain but the school doesn't listen. They don't know how much it affects you. I think it frightens you, it really frightens you. Being put through the traumas of it.*

Her mother also commented on Sophie's experiences of having to read out loud:

*And they've done it time and time again ... and when she comes home she's so upset. She gets stressed out. She cries. The first few times she did it she was so frightened she just burst into tears and was completely humiliated.* (Riddick 1996: 182)

Part of the problem in this situation is that a high number of supply teachers had been used who didn't know about Sophie's reading difficulties. But it does suggest that all teachers need to think about their approach to asking children to read out loud. One teacher, for example, only asked children who volunteered to read out loud but would then ask another child to summarise or pick out the main points from the passage that had been read out. It is also important to distinguish between different types of tasks and to give to those dyslexic children who desire it an opportunity to speak or perform.

*Now, if you said to Sophie 'Oh tomorrow you've got to stand and talk on something' oh she'd love it. She'd stand in front of the class and she'd do it. She'd revel in it. Yes, it seems that one thing is different from the other.*

It can be helpful to encourage individual children or groups of children to talk about the sort of things that really upset them or they really dread having to do in school. Some of these can be quite surprising and can depend very much on the context in which they are presented. One teacher found for example that some children on the earlier books in a reading scheme disliked having to take them home in transparent plastic folders because they were so publicly visible to other children. Simply swapping to opaque folders made them feel less embarrassed.

Mackay argues that for literacy tasks such as spelling it is stressful for dyslexic children to be expected to get 100 per cent. He suggests it is much better to set up an achievable goal such as 7 out of 10, where children can take pride in achieving or even exceeding their target but at the same time learn from their mistakes. 'Target setting with in built margins for error give an important message to all learners about the excitement of "high challenge, low stress" learning opportunities during which mistakes are expected, accepted and valued as evidence that someone has tried' (Mackay 2002: 224).

It is also important to clearly signal to a dyslexic child when speed or imagination or wide vocabulary is required in writing and when the emphasis has to be on accurate spelling and neat handwriting and layout. Generally children should be encouraged to use a wide vocabulary in their writing rather than limiting themselves in order not to make spelling mistakes. Many dyslexic children and students quite explicitly adopt a strategy of not using words they are unsure how to spell. As these often tend to be longer, less frequently used words, or words with an irregular spelling, it can make their work appear more simplistic and less sophisticated than their peers.

## Do

- Try and understand what lies behind poor literacy or numeracy performance.
- Praise child and make them feel a valued member of the class.
- Organise teaching to reduce visible public indicators of difficulty (e.g. reading scheme book in opaque rather than transparent folder).
- Use a range of teaching methods which allow child to participate in class learning.
- Mark work separately for content and appearance.
- Give constructive specific comments on how child can improve spelling, etc.
- Identify child's skills and talents and give opportunities to use them.
- Believe in the child's ability to learn and have high expectations.
- Appreciate amount of effort child puts into literacy tasks.
- Help the child develop positive attributions (I have lots of good ideas; writing lots isn't that important, it's what you say that matters).
- Consult the child about how private or public they would like any support to be.
- Be positive about dyslexia and dyslexic role models.
- Work on specific targeted literacy skills which give child an experience of success.

## Dyslexia as a label

The issues around using a label within the school context are complex and contentious. Educationalists are rightly wary of the negative effects of formal labels like dyslexia or specific learning difficulties within the school environment. But many such children feel they have already been informally labelled as slow or lazy or thick and some think that a label like dyslexia is preferable because it counters these assumptions.

*I'm not branded as thick now.*

*I'm glad I'm called dyslexic rather than lazy.*

103

What is important is that this is discussed privately with children and their parents. Where an identified child and their parents wish the label to be used this should be respected. In some cases a child may find the label helpful at a private level but not want it used in public settings. Many children find it helpful in terms of personal understanding and making sense of a puzzling and sometimes bewildering set of learning experiences. On the other hand some do not want the label used publicly at school because of fear of teasing and discrimination by other children. However, some older children and students feel that a more dyslexia friendly environment should be created which educates people in a positive way about what dyslexia means. At present, negotiating what dyslexia means often seems to be left to parents or specialist dyslexia teachers. What dyslexia means to a child may well change with age and context; some are indifferent or resentful of the label whereas others find it very helpful and supportive.

Carl explained that when he was first given the label he wasn't sure what it meant but went on to talk about how his views on dyslexia were formed.

> *Well, what it was, I had a teacher in that school over there, Mrs Warren, she diagnosed it like she thought I was dyslexic so she told my mum and dad what it was and they told me and then went to get some tests done and then I got told there really.*
>
> *Q: Did it make sense to you at the time?*
>
> *A: In the middle really, I wasn't really too sure (yes, not sure, no).*
>
> *Q: Do you feel now that you've got a clearer idea of what it means?*
>
> *A: A lot clearer.*
>
> *Q: What do you think has made it clearer?*
>
> *A: Mostly it is like people telling me what it is, like teachers and my mum and dad and there are a lot of programmes on television that will come on every now and again.*

Even when children have been clearly identified as having dyslexia or specific learning difficulties, in some schools there is great caution about discussing or acknowledging this. Where children have a positive explanation of what dyslexia means they are less likely to see themselves as a slow learner or stupid (these are terms some of the children we have spoken to use to describe themselves when they do not have a clear picture of what dyslexia means).

As part of valuing diversity and promoting social justice, schools can create an informed climate about dyslexia as one of a number of valued differences between individuals, rather than something equivocal and embarrassing that needs to be hidden away or ignored. Children with dyslexia should at least be given the choice whether they want to consciously use the label dyslexia or ignore it in their daily lives. There are a number of videos and TV programmes now explaining what dyslexia is, and some children find these very helpful, especially if viewed with a sympathetic adult.

## *Role models*

When dyslexic children were asked what they thought about dyslexic role models the vast majority said they found them helpful (Riddick 1996). Nearly all the children who were interviewed had a clear picture of themselves as dyslexic, and were therefore able to identify with dyslexic role models. This may not apply to children who are less clear about what dyslexia means and how it relates to them. Several children also cited a dyslexic parent or relative as a positive role model. Many children will have dyslexic relatives and it can be encouraging for dyslexic parents who sometimes feel they are to 'blame' to know that they can be a positive role model for their child.

Dyslexic students who have left the school or are in the last few years of school can be invited to act as role models or mentors to younger children. Lewis (1995), who was involved in the setting up of specialist dyslexia support in a mainstream comprehensive, commented on the advantage of being able to use older dyslexic students as role models.

Dyslexic children between themselves are good at coming up with the names of dyslexic adults. One school encouraged a group of dyslexic children to make a display on dyslexia including adult role models. These are a list of some of the names that are often mentioned. Although there is dispute over whether some of the historical figures would fit all the criteria for dyslexia, they all seemed to have had unusual learning profiles and some literacy difficulties at school.

| | |
|---|---|
| Albert Einstein (scientist) | Tom Cruise (actor) |
| Ruby Wax (comedienne) | W. B. Yeats (poet) |
| Michael Faraday (scientist) | Cher (singer) |
| Winston Churchill (politician) | Susan Hampshire (actor) |
| Michael Heseltine (politician) | Duncan Goodhew (swimmer) |
| Richard Branson (businessman) | Jackie Stewart (racing driver) |
| Richard Rogers (architect) | Steven Redgrave (rower) |

One Year 11 dyslexic girl found reading Susan Hampshire's autobiography particularly helpful. It is useful to have a range of role models including contemporary ones so children can identify with the ones that are most relevant to them.

> *Interviewer:*    *Have you heard about famous or successful adults who are dyslexic?*
>
> *Carl:*    *Yes, Tom Cruise, Cher, there was a president and what-is-his-name Neil out of the Young Ones, Albert Einstein. I think it is helpful because I explain to people I say to them look at all these famous people and they said okay and accept it more.*

The Adult Dyslexia Organisation produces an excellent series of posters of famous adult dyslexics.

## Resources for understanding and identifying with the culture of dyslexia

- Posters.
- Videos and audiotapes (from BDA, Dyslexia Institute, Adult Dyslexia Organisation).
- TV and radio programmes.
- Newspaper and magazine articles.
- Packs from specialist organisations (e.g. BDA, Dyslexia Institute).
- Talks from local or prominent adult dyslexics.
- Support group meetings.
- Autobiographies by dyslexic adults and children.
- Children's fictional books relating to dyslexia.

## Encouraging special skills or talents

Successful adult dyslexics report that the support of their parents and the encouragement of special skills or talents when they were children were essential in helping them to cope and develop. This is an area that school and parents can discuss together and where appropriate include in a child's IEP. Jamie for example took up weight training both in school and outside of school and has just recently competed in the schoolboys' weightlifting championships. Both Jamie and his mother independently reported that this was a great source of pride and self-esteem for him. Some dyslexic children, perhaps because of their coordination problems and lack of self-esteem when younger, do not make a confident start in sports like football or netball but later on can excel in sports or activities that start at a later age or require a different range of skills. By offering a diverse range of learning experiences and extra-curricular activities, schools can maximise the chance of a child finding an area they can feel confident in. Some dyslexic children, because of low self-esteem and a desire to make themselves invisible and not risk failure, need encouragement and support to get them to try out new activities.

Chapter 6

# Working with Parents and Voluntary Organisations

The last 20 years have seen many changes in society and in education and the voices of parents have also changed (Atkin *et al.* 1988). Current work on school improvement clearly shows (Mortimore *et al.* 1995) that the most effective schools, regardless of the age of pupils or differences in pupil entry, have certain characteristics. In every case, good quality home–school work is a key ingredient.

'It is the parents' unreasonable commitment to their child that makes them good parents' (Anon, cited in Gascoigne 1995). Nowhere is this more important than the area of children with special educational needs, when parents' commitment to their child is at times above and beyond what is normally expected from a parent. The present identification of children's special educational needs and the co-option of remedial measures has in part been brought about by parents striving for an improved education to meet the needs of their child. Scott *et al.* (1992) found that successful adults with dyslexia said the support of their parents during childhood was fundamental to their success. In interviews with dyslexic university students Riddick *et al.* (1997) found the support of parents during their school years was a critical protective factor in how the students were faring. Dyson and Skidmore (1994) found that where comprehensive schools were supportive of children with specific learning difficulties/dyslexia there were generally good relations between school and home, with little conflict. Combined with the findings of improved parental satisfaction in Swansea's dyslexia friendly LEA (see Chapter 1 for details), this indicates that where support for dyslexic children is good, teachers and parents are more likely to form a positive partnership.

*Setting up good parent–teacher relations*

To enable children with dyslexia to reach their potential the following is to be commended:

- Training for professionals involved in this area
- Contact between the parents and teachers
- An acceptance that by working together the children will have encouragement to achieve
- Involve the child in discussions and decisions which are to be made.

(Wolfe 2001)

The National Association for Special Educational Needs (NASEN) published a policy document in March 2000 on 'Partnership with Parents'. The policy states that the positive role and contribution of parents has only recently been recognised in the educational context. The prevailing professional ethos for many years was that parents were more often uninterested in, and at worst could be a hindrance to, their children's education.

The need for a professional shift in ethos when dealing with parents is clearly stated. NASEN continues: 'the partnership has even more relevance and importance to the education of children with special educational needs'. NASEN writes that the key principles in parent partnership are:

- Parental rights
- Parental responsibilities
- Parity in partnership
- Empowerment
- Effective communication
- Support
- Diversity.

## The new Code of Practice

Partnership with parents plays a key role in promoting a culture of cooperation between parents, schools, LEAs and others. This is important in enabling children and young people with SEN to achieve their potential.

All parents of children with special educational needs should be treated as partners. They should be supported so as to be able and empowered to:

- Recognise and fulfil their responsibilities as parents and play an active and valued role in their children's education
- Have knowledge of their child's entitlement within the framework

- Make their views known about how their child is educated
- Have access to information, advice and support during assessment and any related decision-making about special educational provision.

(DfES 2001)

The code continues to say these partnerships can be challenging, requiring positive attitudes by all, and in some circumstances additional support and encouragement for parents.

The relationship between parents and school will depend on a number of individual factors including the age/stage of education a child is at:

*Supporting parents*

- *Nursery–Preschool*: Regular daily contact often involving exchange of information
- *Primary School*: Daily contact tends to diminish over the primary years
- *Secondary School*: Main contact through parents' evenings and formal meetings.

Riddick (1996) carried out interviews with 24 parents of dyslexic children. The parents listed the following as key issues in home–school relations:

- concerns that parents had over child's early reading difficulties were listened to;
- need early support in identifying and understanding the child's difficulties;
- clear suggestions on how they could support their children at home;
- not being made to feel they were to 'blame' in some way;
- clear communication between school and home so problems could be solved;
- open acceptance of the 'D' word (i.e. dyslexia) by school;
- difficulties effectively communicating child's problem at secondary school.

Most parents really wanted support when they first thought there was a problem. This usually arose when children started formal schooling and often centred, initially, on lack of progress in reading. This frequently led to children becoming distressed and upset when asked to read or generally unhappy about attending school. Parents found themselves in a dilemma: the school wanted them to read with their children, but their children hated doing it!

> *Over the years it was terrible, it was traumatic. They just don't want to read books.*

> *Oh, hated it. Mention reading a book and there were tears and all sorts. (Riddick 1996: 72)*

Many parents encountered conflicting views from different professionals and over half of them thought the school was dismissive when they first asked tentatively if their child might be dyslexic. Hopefully with better early identification and support this should become less common, but it does underline the need to take parental concerns seriously and not assume parents are being overanxious.

> *I thought something was up. I was told I was an overprotective mother and Dean was just a slow learner and there was nothing wrong.*

Parents were keen, especially at these early stages, for guidance on how they could support their children. Whereas some parents felt that they were given guidance, many felt that they were left to their own devices and had to struggle on as best they could.

> *I was on my own really, they didn't give me any advice.*

> *I had a lot of contact with the school and to be honest they were quite good.*

Often parents contacted specialist dyslexia organisations for support and for the majority this was their main form of help and guidance. Parents particularly valued the chance to meet other parents through these organisations and found this a vital form of support over the years. Meetings or forums in school which allow parents of children with special needs to meet should therefore be encouraged. Advice on specific structured support for younger children is often very welcome. Parents vary considerably in their commitments so this should always be offered in an appropriate form and should not make parents feel inadequate or ineffectual. The vast majority of parents interviewed found there were difficulties at times in trying to get their children to do extra literacy work at home, so reassure parents that it is a very common problem. Discuss other ways they can support their children by helping them relax, learn from outings, hobbies, being read to, discussing TV programmes, etc.

Just over half the parents interviewed felt that the school 'blamed' them in some way for their child's difficulties, most commonly by suggesting they were overanxious or neurotic. This may not have been the message some schools or teachers intended to convey but it does emphasise the need for a non-judgemental and open approach with parents.

Where parents do feel they have a working partnership with the school and they can see that real attempts are being made to meet their child's needs, they are often delighted by these:

*We were so pleased with what they have done for him, we wrote a letter to the head thanking him and all the teachers that had really helped him.*

As children get older and there is less informal contact so different methods for working with parents need to be developed. The main difficulty parents encountered at secondary school was that even when there was a good special needs department, subject teachers often didn't seem to know about their child's difficulties. Many schools would acknowledge that with large numbers of teachers and children effective communication is a problem, although IEPs would be seen as part of the solution.

The SENCO in one comprehensive has run parents' evenings addressing the booster lessons in Year 7, the New Code of Practice, study skills in Year 9 and the SATs. These informal presentations and discussions can inform parents and dispel fears. Not all parents will be able to attend such events but even if attendance is low initially there are often long-term benefits. The networking of parents that do attend will help ensure that the word is quickly spread. As parents become confident in a school's open approach to them, they will be enabled to take part in the education of their child.

## Transfer to secondary school

Most parents tend to be worried about the transfer from primary to secondary school. Parents of children with special educational needs in particular have concerns about what is going to happen. Are their needs going to be met? Are they going to cope in mainstream school? They have a fear of the child being sent to special school if he or she cannot cope or is not supported and forming the necessary new relationships with many more staff.

The first meeting between teachers and parents at an annual review at a primary school, or an initial visit on an open night is important, as first impressions are valuable in building a relationship. Care and sensitivity are required at annual reviews as discussions can damage as well as foster relationships between home and school. It is therefore essential to foster cooperation between the parents, the school and teachers. If a school wants parents to support it and their child's education, it will be necessary to find out from them what they would like to have implemented. Some parents may have serious problems themselves and need helping. Their memories of school may not be happy, they may feel intimidated by the ethos, and neutral territory may have to be made available before the school can establish what is in the child's best interests from the parents' viewpoint.

If there is a family history of literacy difficulties the family may well be ashamed of it and you will be given a 'vague history'. Indeed many family members may not have been picked up at all as having difficulties, or if picked up may never have overcome fully the earlier shaming experiences they had at school. And that family member may well have passed on survival techniques for the dyslexic to get on in the overly written/literary world in school where they are expected to try and survive.

## *Consulting parents on assessment and IEPs*

Parents have a great deal of information which, if shared with professionals, can be to the benefit of all working with a child. However, a school is a very busy place and time must be set aside to enable reviews to take place. This will vary from school to school. For example, in one comprehensive the parents' evening is used for one review and the school gives the SENCO time off timetable to complete a second review.

In this same school reviews of children who are causing concern to parents, teachers or other agencies are held more regularly as needs dictate. The reviews take place with the child present if at all possible. This allows everyone concerned to discuss provision which has taken place, difficulties which may have arisen or any issues such as whether targets have been met, future targets and provisions to meet the needs of the child. These discussions must not be dominated by the teacher, in fact the teacher should actively listen and ask questions.

Parents become anxious if professionals do not accept their concerns. If there are inconsistent views between different teachers about the child's learning problems, the parents' evening becomes a depressing and sometimes tearful experience. No wonder some parents are never seen at parents' evenings. Parents worry about their child's future. How will they cope with GCSEs? Will they get a job? A family may be only too aware of other family members being disadvantaged by continuing dyslexia problems.

It has been found that parents' knowledge of Special Educational Needs statutory requirements and provision in schools is limited. This is not a criticism of the parents but more so of the schools for failing to inform parents of procedures and their rights. Schools can address this by holding informal presentations on procedures in the school, giving parents copies of 'Special Educational Needs: a Guide for Parents', available from DfES, and the telephone number for the Code of Practice which is free of charge: 0845 602 2260.

Parents should be proactive in making sure that their child's learning difficulties are being properly addressed. Parents have a crucial role to play in providing support for their dyslexic child. They should:

*Parental role and responsibility*

- alert relevant staff at school if there is a concern, however small;
- help their child in all aspects of organisation;
- help as much as possible, and whenever practical, with homework, and let staff at school know if there are difficulties in this area;
- alert teachers to time spent doing homework; try to keep this to a reasonable time limit so life is not all schoolwork and catch-up lessons;
- be as positive, encouraging and optimistic as possible;
- contribute to the child's IEP.

Access to a telephone is important for communication as it can frequently be used to follow up any written correspondence. This gives an opportunity to discuss the correspondence and explain the contents when necessary.

**What can parents do to help?**

Look for gradual improvement. Don't rush your child. If the work seems very simple, it's because it is better to have a good foundation than have gaps in knowledge or skills.

You could also read to him and let him read to you. Your child's teacher, the educational psychologist or a specialist teacher might give you information about a technique called 'paired reading', which can often help.

Give your child lots of encouragement and praise – remembering that he will probably get very frustrated and disheartened.

You can get advice on dyslexia from a number of places and the school can direct you towards help with the following:

- literacy support and homework;
- organisation, especially of homework, equipment, and deadlines for course work;
- proofreading work;
- how to be a role model for reading;
- listening and encouraging.

The importance of parents' involvement and rights under the Code of Practice has helped change the teacher's role. Providing parents with information where they can seek help and advice regarding their child's education can be mutually beneficial. School can be a disheartening experience. Make home a safe and encouraging place:

- Encourage any particular talents that your child exhibits such as art, sport or music. Bring to the child's attention successful dyslexics. Dyslexic children should be helped to feel they can succeed in at least one area of their life.

  *He loves cooking. I think that's a real outlet for him.*

- Never discuss your child's learning difficulties in front of him without including him in the discussion, or behind closed doors when he may be listening. Praising your child encourages positive behaviour. Remember the child is more normal than different. Emphasise his strengths and particular abilities.
- Be prepared to make time to back up homework or organise school bags.
- Keep regularly in touch with the teachers: involve them in helping your child's peer group understand what it is to be dyslexic and how they can help.
- Colour code all books and bags so that your child recognises them instantly. It works!
- Teach your child how to pack and unpack a school bag and organise his pencil case. Do not assume that he will naturally acquire these skills.
- Keep a record of how long homework takes and share this information with the teacher, who may be unaware of how much time your child needs.

### Strategies

- Read assigned books or material to, or with, your child. Knowledge and understanding are important, so explain the meaning of new words and explain what is going on in the text.

- If the use of conventional dictionaries and diaries is too difficult or time consuming, explore and teach the use of ACE spelling dictionary, electronic tools, such as electronic organisers and spellcheck, dictionary and appointment-calendar software.
- Adopt a common-sense approach. If a child asks for help with spelling or grammar when he is writing, give him the answer and let him get on with his work. This applies equally with maths; dyslexic children often have problems with rote memory. Supply the answer if he knows the process.
- Make time to listen to your child and give the opportunity in a calm atmosphere to tell you what happened during the day or what his or her concerns are. Sharing problems with a sympathetic listener can make them seem much less burdensome.
- Find out about support groups and other relevant organisations in your area. It is often a great relief to know that your family is not alone in helping a child with learning difficulties, and you will receive a lot of helpful information and support.
- Parents feel their child benefits from using the school diary to record homework. The parents are able to comment on homework as well as look at what is to be completed.

The SEN Code of Practice states that:

*Parents hold key information and have a critical role to play in their children's education. There are strong reasons for working in partnership with all parents. If they feel confident that schools and professionals actively involve them, take account of their wishes, feelings and unique perspectives on their children's development, then the work of those schools and professionals can be more effective.*

## Gaining the families' perspective and experience of dyslexia

Good practice in the management of special educational needs requires that schools enter into a partnership with parents based upon mutual trust and collaboration. Such a partnership may not always be easily achieved. Parents know their own child best. If schools view parents as valuable partners, this often provides a springboard for the child, so everyone benefits.

Many parents of pupils with special educational needs will, understandably, have concerns and anxieties about their child. Schools should start to consult parents as soon as there are any concerns about the child's learning problems. If at a later stage concerns become greater, parents are more likely to trust that the school is doing its best because it has already pointed out the difficulties. Schools need to be aware of parents' apprehensions and to create an atmosphere in which they feel assured and comfortable. The ways in which meetings are conducted can have a major impact upon the ways in which parents view the school.

As regards the supply of information, schools can play an important role in what should ideally be a two-way process. Schools may find it necessary to provide help to parents in the writing of reports, or may accept a verbal report instead. In all dealings with parents, assumptions should not be made:

- That written information can be read.
- That the language contained in documents has been understood.
- That information is interpreted in the way that it was intended.
- That parents/carers have all of the background know-ledge/information to interpret a document.
- That parents hear good news as well as not such good news.
- That cultural differences have been taken into account.

Parents and children are to be involved in the planning related to Individual Education Plans (IEPs). This should mean ideally that parents are involved in both the target setting process and review of progress. Parents should be provided with copies of the pupil's IEP or PSP (Pastoral Support Plan) prior to any meeting to discuss or alter them. Their views should be sought and parents should be consulted about all aspects of the IEP. Schools should endeavour to involve parents in learning and behaviour target setting, and should ensure that they are aware of the importance of individual targets and why they have been set. Schools should ensure that reports are readily available, and targets are achievable and understood by parents.

Parents have a responsibility to work in collaboration with schools in the delivery of individual education or behaviour programmes. Schools should maintain regular contact with parents and should record the expectations of parents, and the response to requests for help in delivering plans. Many schools have found that a system of home–school diaries has been effective in maintaining regular contact between home and school. For some parents personal or telephone contact may be a more appropriate means of communication.

*The parent partnership service* is able to give parents relevant information, impartial advice and support through a helpline, home visits, attendance at meetings and information leaflets, and to liaise with SEN officers and schools on behalf of parents.

## Where will the meeting take place?

*Practical suggestions for developing partnership with parents*

If it is in a classroom ensure that all chairs are the same height and that the teacher does not sit behind their desk as this is off-putting for the parents. A round table is preferred but not always possible.

Offer a suggestion to meet the parents on mutual territory as the school may be a threatening environment to a parent. A community centre may have rooms available, or it may be worth considering using EWOs (Educational Welfare Officers) for a home visit.

## Conducting meetings

- Parents are sent documentation to be discussed with an agenda.
- Meetings commence at the appointed time.
- Make parents welcome at the beginning of meetings.
- Everyone is introduced and roles explained.
- Ensure that parents are clear about the purpose of meetings before they take place.
- Provide information about the roles and responsibilities of professionals present in meetings.
- Avoid excessive use of jargon.
- Encourage parents to bring a representative or friend to meetings if desired.
- Provide time for parents to express their feelings, opinions and ideas at the meeting.
- You are open and honest.
- The views of parents are recorded.
- Clarify any decisions that are made at the end of a meeting.
- Provide parents with written minutes or notes as soon after the meeting as possible.
- Provide appropriate support for parents/carers for whom English is an additional language.
- The venue is comfortable and non-threatening.
- The venue is private.

**Written communication**

- Text is kept to a minimum.
- Sentences are short.
- Text is at least size 12 font: Comic Sans is the easiest to read.
- Everyday words are used. Any jargon that cannot be avoided is explained.
- Text is translated into community languages or onto tape or provided in a larger font size where necessary.
- The use of the school diary can be a means of communication.
- Written information is sent home via an appropriate, reliable distribution route (children's bags may not be reliable).
- Written information is sent to families when children are absent.
- The newsletter/letter/report goes out regularly on the same day of the week/month.
- Different coloured paper is used to distinguish between types of communication.

## Liaising with voluntary organisations – the work of the BDA and the Dyslexia Institute

Information is obtainable from the British Dyslexia Association (BDA), which has local branches throughout the country. The BDA is the voice of people with dyslexia. The charity offers advice, information and help to people with dyslexia, their families and professionals who support them. Contact them at 98 London Road, Reading, Berkshire, RG1 5AU. Tel: 01734 668271/2. There is also a national helpline: 0118 966 8271. www.bda-dyslexia.org.uk

Helpliners are frequently asked: How can I find out if my child is dyslexic? Most callers think that their child is dyslexic, sometimes this is because another member of the family is or at least thinks they are. There are a number of adults who telephone for advice too. Schools in some areas pass on national and local helpline telephone numbers and have developed good working relationships. Email is becoming an increased form of communication both nationally and at local level. Schools too may wish to develop the use of email as a form of communication as it allows working parents to contact the school at their convenience.

The Dyslexia Institute is a leading authority on teaching children and adults with dyslexia. The charity provides a national network of 25 main centres and some 130 linked learning centres. All DI centres offer assessment and individual and small-group teaching. Many centres also work closely with their local education authorities and other agencies to train teachers and improve awareness of the needs of dyslexic people. For further information on the Dyslexia Institute the address is 133 Gresham Road, Staines, Middlesex, TW18 2AJ. Tel: 01784 463851. www.dyslexia-inst.org.uk

## Supporting and enabling parents

Teachers, schools and parents ought to form an alliance working for the best interests of the children and their educational development. The children have a central part to play in this, particularly as they progress through secondary school and become young adults.

There are many ways this can be done: open discussion sharing ideas, relaxed meetings, passing on information about local dyslexia groups and other groups such as network 81 and IPSEA.

The key to all of this is respect for each party involved and a focus on the child's needs.

# References and Resources

Adams, M. J. (1990) *Beginning to Read: Thinking and learning about print*. Cambridge, MA: MIT Press.

Alexander, R. (1992) *Policy and Practice in Primary Education*. London: Routledge.

Ashton, C. (2001) 'Assessment and support in secondary schools: an educational psychologist's perspective', in L. Peer and G. Reid (eds) *Dyslexia-Successful Inclusion in the Secondary School*. London: David Fulton Publishers.

Atkin, J., Bastiani, J. and Good, J. (1988) *Listening to Parents: An approach to improvement of home–school relations*. London: Croom Helm.

Basic Skills Agency (1997) *Does Numeracy Matter?* London: Basic Skills Agency.

Battle, J. (1992) *Culture-Free Self-esteem Inventories*. Austin, TX: PRO-ED.

Beech, J. R. (1997) 'Assessment of memory and reading', in J. Beech and C. Singleton (eds) *The Psychological Assessment of Reading*. London: Routledge.

Berninger, V. (2001) 'Understanding the "lexia" in dyslexia', *Annals of Dyslexia*, **51**, 23–48.

Bradley, L. L. and Bryant, P. E. (1983) 'Categorising sounds and learning to read: a causal connection', *Nature*, **301**, 419–521.

British Dyslexia Association (2000) *Achieving Dyslexia Friendly Schools*. Reading: BDA.

British Dyslexia Asssociation (2002) *BDA Handbook*. Reading: BDA.

British Psychological Society (1999) *Dyslexia, Literacy and Psychological Assessment*. Report of a working party of the Division of Educational and Child Psychology. Leicester: BPS.

Brooks, P. and Weeks, S. (1999) *Individual Styles in Learning to*

*Spell: Improving Spelling in Children with Literacy Difficulties and All Children in Mainstream Schools*. Nottingham: DfEE.

Brooks, P., Everatt, J. and Weeks, S. (2001) 'Spelling progress can be doubled', *Special Children Magazine*, April, 32–3.

Butkowsky, I. S. and Willows, D. M. (1980) 'Cognitive-motivational characteristics of children varying in reading ability; evidence of learned helplessness in poor readers', *Journal of Educational Psychology*, 72, **3**, 408–22.

Buzan, T. (1993) *The Mind Map Book: Radiant thinking*. London: BBC Books.

Byrne, B. (1998) *The Foundation of Literacy: The Child's Acquisition of the Alphabetic Principle*. Mahweh, NJ: Lawrence Erlbaum Associates.

Campione, J. C., Shapiro, A. M. and Brown, A. L. (1995) 'Forms of transfer in a community of learners: flexible learning and understanding', in A. McKeough, J. Lupart and A. Marini (eds) *Teaching for Transfer*. Hillsdale, NJ: Lawrence Erlbaum Associates.

Casey, R., Levy, S., Brown, K. and Brooks-Gunn, J. (1992) 'Impaired emotional health in children with mild reading disability', *Developmental and Behavioural Paediatrics* 13, **4**, 256–60.

Coopersmith, S. (1967) *The Antecedents of Self-Esteem*. San Francisco, CA: W. H. Freeman.

Cunningham, A. E. and Stanovich, K. E. (1998) 'What reading does for the mind', *American Educator*, 22, Spring/Summer, 8–15.

de Shazer, S. (1988) *Clues: Investigating Solutions in Brief Therapy*. New York: Norton.

de Shazer, S. (1994) *Words Were Originally Magic*. New York: Norton.

Deponio, P., Landon, K., Mullin, K. and Reid, G. (2000) 'An audit of the processes involved in identifying and assessing bilingual learners suspected of being dyslexic: a Scottish study', *Dyslexia – An International Journal of Research and Practice*, **6**, 1, 29–41.

DfEE (1997) *Excellence for all Schools* (Green Paper). London: The Stationery Office.

DfES (2001) *Special Educational Needs – Code of Practice*. Nottinghamshire: DfES Publications.

Durham LEA (2001) *Specific Learning Difficulties: Dyslexia and Dyspraxia*. Durham County Council.

Dyson, A. and Skidmore, D. (1994) *Provision for Pupils with Specific Learning Difficulties in School*. A report to SOED (Scottish Office Education Department).

Edwards, J. (1994) *The Scars of Dyslexia*. London: Cassell.

Elbaum, B. and Vaughn, S. (2001) 'School-based interventions to enhance the self-concept of students with learning disabilities: a metaanalysis', *Elementary School Journal*, **101**, 3, 303–29.

Fawcett, A. J. and Nicolson, R. (1992) 'Automatisation deficits in balance for dyslexic children', *Perceptual and Motor Skills*, **75**, 507–29.

Fawcett, A. J. and Nicolson, R. (1996) *The Dyslexia Screening Test*. London: Psychological Corporation.

Fawcett, A. J. and Nicolson, R. (2001) 'Dyslexia and the role of the cerebellum', in A. J. Fawcett (ed.), *Dyslexia: Theory and Good Practice*. London: Whurr.

Fawcett, A. J., Nicolson, R. and Lee, R. (2000) *Baseline Early Skills Tests*. London: The Psychological Corporation.

Feuerstein, R. (1988) 'Mediated learning experience: What makes it powerful?' Chapter 3 from, *Don't accept me as I am: helping 'retarded' people to excel*. London: Plenum Press.

Flavell, J. H., Miller, P. H. and Miller, S. A. (1977) *Cognitive Development*. Upper Saddle River, NJ: Prentice-Hall.

Frederickson, N., Frith, U. and Reason, R. (1997) *Phonological Assessment Battery*. London: NFER–Nelson.

Frith, C. and Frith, U. (1996) 'A biological marker for dyslexia', *Nature*, 382, 19–20.

Frith, U. (1985) 'Beneath the surface of developmental dyslexia', in K. E. Patterson, J. C. Marshall and M. Coltheart (eds), *Surface Dyslexia*. London: Lawrence Erlbaum.

Frith, U. (1992) 'Cognitive development and cognitive deficit', *The Psychologist*, **5**, 1, 13–19.

Frith, U. (1995) 'Can we have a shared theoretical framework?', *Educational and Child Psychology*, **12**, 8.

Garzia, R. (1993) 'Optometric factors in reading disability', in D. M. Willows (ed.), *Visual Processes in Reading and Reading Disabilities*. NJ: Lawrence Erlbaum.

Gascoigne, E. (1995) *Working with Parents as Partners in SEN*. London: David Fulton.

Gathercole, S. and Baddley, A. (1996) *The Children's Test of Nonword Repetition*. London: Psychological Corporation.

Gillingham, A. and Stillman, B. (1956) *Remedial Training for Children with Specific Disability in Reading, Spelling and Penmanship*. Cambridge: MA Educators Publishing Service.

Gjessing, H. J. and Karlsen, B. (1989) *A Longitudinal Study of Dyslexia*. New York: Harper and Row.

Harter, S. (1985) *Manual for the Self-Perception Profile for Children*. Denver: University of Denver.

Hatcher, P. J. (1994) *Sound Linkage: An integrated programme for overcoming reading difficulties*. London: Whurr.

Hemmings, P. (1991) *All About Me*. Barnardo's.

Hilsdon, E., Jackson, N., Lumsdon, D. B., Nicholson, D. and Verney, J. (2002) *Sounds in Words*. Northumberland County Council.

Hornsby, B. and Farmer, M. (1990) 'Some effects of a dyslexia-centred teaching programme', in P. D. Pumfry and C. D. Elliott (eds), *Children's Difficulties in Reading, Spelling and Writing*. London: Falmer Press.

Hornsby, B. and Miles, T. R. (1980) 'The effects of a dyslexic-centred teaching programme', *British Journal of Educational Psychology*, **50**, 3, 236–42.

Hulme, C., Muter, V. and Snowling, M. (1998) 'Segmentation does predict early progress in reading better than rhyme: a reply to Bryant', *Journal of Experimental Child Psychology*.

Humphrey, N. (2002) 'Self-concept and Self-esteem in developmental dyslexia', *British Journal of Special Education*, **29**, 1, 29–36.

Johnson, M., Peer, L. and Lee, R. (2001) 'Pre-school children and dyslexia: policy, identification and intervention', in Fawcett, A. (ed.), *Dyslexia: Theory and Good Practice*. London: Whurr.

Kelly, K. (2002) 'Dyslexia and bi-lingual pupils', in M. Johnson and L. Peer (eds) *The Dyslexia Handbook*. Reading: BDA.

Kosikenin, Blum, Bisson, Phillips, Creamer and Baker (2000) 'Intermittent conductive hearing loss and language development', in D. Bishop and K. Mogford (eds), *Language Development in Exceptional Circumstances*. Hove: Lawrence Erlbaum Associates.

Law, J., Boyle, J., Harris, F., Harkness, A. and Nye, C. (1998) 'Screening for speech and language delay', *Health Technology Assessment* **2**, 9, 35–42.

Lawrence, D. (1987) *Enhancing Self-Esteem in the Classroom*. London: Paul Chapman.

Layton, L., Deeny, K., Upton, G. and Tall, G. (1996) 'Promoting phonological awareness in preschool children', in M. Snowling and J. Stackhouse (eds), *Dyslexia, Speech and Language: A Practitioner's Handbook*. London: Whurr.

Lewandowski, L. and Arcangelo, K. (1994) 'The social adjustment and self-concept of adults with learning disabilities', *Journal of Learning Disabilities* **27**, 598–605.

Lewis, J. (1995) 'The development of a unit for dyslexic children in a British comprehensive school', *Dyslexia – An International Journal of Research and Practice*, **1**, 1.

Lundberg, I. and Hoien, T. (2001) 'Dyslexia and phonology', in A. Fawcett (ed.) *Dyslexia: Theory and Good Practice*. London: Whurr.

Mackay, N. (2001) 'Dyslexia friendly schools', in L. Peer and G. Reid, *Dyslexia-Successful Inclusion in the Secondary School*. London: David Fulton Publishers.

Mackay, N. (2002) 'The 4 rules of spelling: a pragmatic approach for non-specialists', in M. Johnson and L. Peer (eds), *The Dyslexia Handbook 2002*. Reading: BDA.

Marsh, H. (1990) *Self-Description Questionnaire*. Sydney: University of Western Sydney.

McLoughlin, D., Fitzgibbon, G. and Young, V. (1994) *Adult Dyslexia: Assessment, counselling and training*. London: Whurr.

Miles, T. and Miles, E. (1999) *Dyslexia: A hundred years on*. (2nd edition). Buckingham: OU Press.

Mortimore, P., Hillman, J. and Sammons, P. (1995) 'Key characteristics of effective schools: a review of school effectiveness research'. London: London Institute of Education (published for OFSTED).

Moss, H. and Reason, R. (1998) 'Interactive group work with young children needing additional help in learning to read', *Support for Learning*, **13**, 1.

Muter, V., Hulme, C. and Snowling, M. (1997) *Phonological Abilities Test*. London: Psychological Corporation.

National Association for Special Educational Needs (2000) *Partnership with Parents*. NASEN.

Nicolson, R. and Fawcett, A. (1996) *The Dyslexia Early Screening Test*. London: Psychological Corporation.

Northumberland County Council (1995) *Special Educational Needs Assistants and Teachers (SENAT)*.

Northumberland County Council (2002) SNIPP Plus.

OFSTED (1999) *Pupils with Specific Learning Difficulties in Mainstream Schools*. London: OFSTED Publications Centre.

Peer, L. (1994) *Dyslexia: The Training and Awareness of Teachers*. Reading: British Dyslexia Association.

Pietrowski, J. and Reason, R. (2000) 'The National Literacy Strategy and Dyslexia: A comparison of teaching methods and materials', *Support for Learning*, **15**, 51–7.

Pine, J. (1994) 'The language of primary care givers', in C. Galloway and B. Richards (eds), *Input and Interaction in Language Aquisition*. Cambridge: Cambridge University Press.

Pollock, J. and Waller, E. (1994) *Day-to-Day Dyslexia in the Classroom*. London: Routledge.

Reid, G. (1998) *Dyslexia: A Practitioner's Handbook*. Chichester: Wiley.

Rhodes, J. and Ajmal, Y. (1995) *Solution Focused Thinking in Schools*. London: BT Press.

Riddick, B. (1996) *Living with Dyslexia: The social and emotional consequences of specific learning difficulties*. London: Routledge.

Riddick, B. (2000) 'An examination of the relationship between labelling and stigmatisation with special reference to dyslexia', *Disability and Society*, **15**, 4, 653–67.

Riddick, B., Farmer, M. and Sterling, C. (1997) *Students and Dyslexia; Growing up with a specific learning difficulty.* London: Whurr.

Riddick, B., Sterling, C., Farmer, M. and Morgan, S. (1999) 'Self-esteem and anxiety in the educational histories of adult dyslexic students', *Dyslexia*, **5**, 227–48.

Ripley, K., Daines, B. and Barrett, J. (1997) *Dyspraxia: A Guide for Teachers and Parents*. London: David Fulton Publishers.

Rosenthal, J. (1973) 'Self-esteem in dyslexic children', *Academic Therapy*, **9**, 1, 27–39.

Scarborough, H. S. (1990) 'Very early language deficits in dyslexic children', *Child Development*, **61**, 1728–63.

Scott, M. E., Sherman, A. and Phillips, H. (1992) 'Helping individuals with dyslexia succeed in adulthood', *Journal of Instructional Psychology*, **19**, 3.

Singleton, C. (1997) *Computerized Cognitive Profiling System.* Newark, NJ: Chameleon Educational Systems Ltd.

Singleton, C. (1999) 'Dyslexia in Higher Education'. Report of the National Working Party. The University of Hull.

Snowling, M. J. (1987) *Dyslexia: A cognitive developmental perspective.* Oxford: Blackwell.

Snowling, M. J. (1995) 'Phonological processing and developmental dyslexia', *Journal of Research in Reading*, **18**, 132–8.

Snowling, M. and Nation, K. (1997) 'Language, phonology and learning to read', in C. Hulme and M. Snowling (eds) *Dyslexia: Biology, Cognition and Intervention*. London, Whurr Publishers.

Snowling, M., Stothard, S. and MacLean (1996) *Graded Non-word Reading Test.* Bury St Edmunds: Thames Valley Testing Company.

Solity, J. E. (1996) 'Reframing psychological assessment', *Educational and Child Psychology*, **13**, 3, 94–102.

Solity, J. E. and Bull, S. J. (1987) *Special Needs: Bridging the curriculum gap.* Buckingham: Open University Press.

Springett, L. (2002) 'Dyslexia Friendly Schools', in L. Peer and M. Johnson (eds), *The Dyslexia Handbook*. Reading: The British Dyslexia Association.

Stackhouse, J. (2000) 'Barriers to literacy developments in children with speech and language difficulties', in D. Bishop and L. Leonard (eds), *Speech and Language Impairments in Children*. Hove: Psychology Press.

Stanovich, K. E. (1986) 'Matthew effects in reading: some consequences of the individual differences in the acquisition of literacy', *Reading Research Quarterly*, **21**, 360–407.

Stanovich, K. E. and Siegal, L. S. (1994) 'The phenotypic performance profile of reading disabled children', *Journal of Educational Psychology*, **86**, 1–30.

Stein, J. F. and Walsh, V. (1997) 'To see but not to read: the magnocellular theory of dyslexia', *Trends in Neurological Science,* **20**, 4, 147–52.

Swanson, H. L. (1999) 'Reading research for students with LD: a meta-analysis of intervention outcomes', *Journal of Learning Disabilities,* **32**, 504–32.

Thomson, M. (1990) *Dyslexia and Development* (3rd edition). London: Whurr.

Thomson, M. and Hartley, G. M. (1980) 'Self-esteem in dyslexic children', *Academic Therapy,* **16**, 1, 19–36.

*Times Educational Supplement (2001)* July 13, p. 4.

Tod, J. (1999) *IEPs – Dyslexia.* London: David Fulton Publishers.

Torgesen, J. K. (2001) 'The theory and practice of intervention: comparing outcomes from prevention and remediation studies', in A. Fawcett (ed.), *Dyslexia: Theory and Good Practice.* London: Whurr Publishers.

Wade, J. and Moore, B. (1998) 'An early start with books, literacy and mathematics: evidence from a longitudinal study', *Educational Review* **50**, 134–45.

Wolf, M. and O'Brien, B. (2001) 'On issues of time, fluency and intervention', in A. J. Fawcett (ed.), *Dyslexia: Theory and Good Practice.* London: Whurr.

Wolfe, J. (2001) 'Working with parents in the secondary school'. Unpublished dissertation available from Sunderland University.

Wood, J., Wright, J. and Stackhouse, J. (2000) *Language and Literacy: Joining Together.* Reading: British Dyslexia Association.

## Available computer tests

Instines The Smart (age 12+) Computer-based screening for dyslexia.
Telephone: 0771 572 5090 www.DyslexiaAssessments.com

LASS Secondary Computerised, multifunctional assessment for students of all abilities (normed for 11–15-year-olds), Lucid Research Ltd, PO Box 63, Beverley, East Yorkshire HU17 8ZZ www. lucid-research. com

## Further help and advice

The Joint Council for General Qualifications GCE, VCE, GCSE and GNVQ: Regulations and guidance relating to candidates with particular requirements. Obtainable from The Joint Council for General Qualifications, 1 Regent Street, Cambridge CB2 1GG.

*List of useful website addresses*

Adult Dyslexia Organisation: email: dyslexia@dial.pipex.com

British Dyslexia Association: www.bda-dyslexia.org.uk

Dyslexia Information: www.dyslexia-information.com

Dyslexia Institute: www.dyslexia-inst.org.uk

Dyslexia Unit Bangor: www.dyslexia.bangor.ac.uk

European Dyslexia Association: www.eda.en.com

Homeschooling dyslexic children: www.dyslexics.org.uk

Homework support: www.dyslexiasupport.co.uk

Hornsby International Dyslexia Centre: www.hornsby.co.uk

Iansyst SEN Technology: www.dyslexic.com

International Dyslexia Association (formally Orton DS): www.interdys.org

National Grid for Learning: http://inclusion.ngfl.gov.uk

National Internet Accessibility Database: http://niad.disinhe.ac.uk

PATOSS The Professional Association of Teachers of Students with SpLD: www.patoss-dyslexia.org

Scottish Dyslexia Trust: www.dyslexia-scotland.org

Study skills: www.calsc.co.uk

www.dyslexiahelp.co.uk

Written by an 11-year-old-boy: www.iamdyslexic.com

www.dyslexia-net.co.uk – This site is aimed at teenagers as well.

A dyslexia website for children: www.dyslexicfriends.co.uk

A website on famous dyslexics and a link to their biography on line: www.playback.net/dyslexia

You will also find information about children who are visual-spatial learners at www.gifteddevelopment.com and www.dyslexic.com

Wordswork: a favourite interactive program for individual students and resource centres. More information at www.dyslexic.com/wordwork.htm

The Clifton Press disk of html reference material. Information at: www.dyslexic.com/study.htm

www.dyslexic.com/language.htm

www.vtc.ngfl.gov.uk/docserver.php?docid=1945

www.cast.org/ncac/ supports inclusion for young people with dyslexia 'National Center on Accessing the General Curriculum'.

## *Books on-line*

sen.marketing@ukonline.co.uk

www.whurr.co.uk

www.crossboweducation.com

www.janpoustie.co.uk

www.fultonpublishers.co.uk

www.brainwise.co.uk/books

The home of the 'educational kinesiology foundation': www.braingym.org

www.zoomlearning.co.uk/bg/index.shtml

Primary movement web: www.primarymovement.org

Anger management: www.cheiron-quietplace.com

Education law: www.ipsea.org.uk.

# Index